EFFECTIVE LEADERSHIP SKILLS FOR MANAGERS

ELEVATE YOUR TEAM WITH CONFIDENCE AND EMPATHY TO INSPIRE, MOTIVATE AND FOSTER A VIBRANT WORKPLACE CULTURE

J.A. LOUGH

CONTENTS

Introduction 7

1. THE SPECTRUM OF LEADERSHIP STYLES—
IDENTIFYING YOURS 11
1.1 The Impact of Emotional Intelligence on Your
Leadership 14
1.2 Adapting Your Leadership Style to Team Needs 17
1.3 Authenticity in Leadership: Being True to Your
Style 21

2. TRANSITIONING FROM PEER TO LEADER 25
2.1 Strategies for Asserting Your New Role
Respectfully 25
2.2 Building Credibility as a New Leader 27
2.3 Handling Resentment and Resistance 30
2.4 Fostering a Culture of Growth as a New Leader 33

3. EFFECTIVE COMMUNICATION—THE
BACKBONE OF LEADERSHIP 37
3.1 Crafting Clear and Inspiring Messages 37
3.2 Active Listening: A Leader's Superpower 40
3.3 Feedback Loops: Encouraging Open Dialogue 43
3.4 Navigating Difficult Conversations With Grace 46

4. LEADING ACROSS CULTURES—THE POWER OF
UNDERSTANDING 51
4.1 Understanding Cultural Differences in
Communication 51
4.2 Adapting Leadership Communication to Remote
Teams 54
4.3 Bridging Generational Gaps in Communication 57
4.4 Creating Inclusive Spaces for All Voices 61

5. ASSEMBLING YOUR DREAM TEAM 65
5.1 Identifying and Leveraging Diverse Strengths 66
5.2 The Role of Trust in Team Performance 68

5.3 Setting Clear Goals and Expectations   72

5.4 Encouraging Innovation and Creative Thinking   75

6. NURTURING TEAM GROWTH AND DEVELOPMENT   79

6.1 Individual Assessments for Personalized Plans   79

6.2 The Power of Constructive Feedback   82

6.3 Facilitating Team Learning Opportunities   85

6.4 Recognizing and Celebrating Team Achievements   88

7. NAVIGATING THE WINDS OF CHANGE   95

7.1 Communicating Change Effectively   95

7.2 Managing Team Emotions During Change   97

7.3 Leading by Example: Modeling Adaptability   99

7.4 Keeping the Team Focused and Motivated   102

8. OVERCOMING LEADERSHIP CHALLENGES   105

8.1. Resolving Conflicts Within the Team   105

8.2. Dealing with Underperformance Constructively   108

8.3. Balancing Leadership and Personal Life   111

8.4. Leading Remote Teams Successfully   115

9. BUILDING YOUR LEADERSHIP IDENTITY   119

9.1. Defining Your Leadership Philosophy   119

9.2. Communicating Your Leadership Vision   123

9.3. The Impact of Leadership on Organizational Culture   126

9.4. Leaving a Lasting Leadership Legacy   130

10. CULTIVATING GROWTH—THE CONTINUOUS EVOLUTION OF LEADERSHIP   133

10.1. Embracing Lifelong Learning in Leadership   133

10.2. Seeking Feedback for Continuous Improvement   136

10.3. The Role of Mentoring in Leadership Development   138

10.4. Staying Ahead of Leadership Trends   141

11. CRAFTING YOUR LEADERSHIP ACTION PLAN   145

11.1. Setting SMART Leadership Goals   145

11.2. Identifying Resources and Support   147

11.3. Creating a Timeline for Your Leadership
Development   149
11.4. Monitoring and Adjusting Your Plan   152

12. PUTTING YOUR LEADERSHIP PLAN INTO
ACTION   155
12.1 45. Taking the First Steps: Initiating Change 155
12.2. Building Momentum and Maintaining Focus   157
12.3. Celebrating Milestones and Reflecting on
Progress   159
12.4. Scaling Your Leadership Impact   162
12.5. Nurturing Future Leaders   165
12.6. Evolving Your Leadership for Future
Challenges   169

Conclusion   173
References   177

INTRODUCTION

Stepping into a leadership role is akin to standing on the edge of a precipice: the view is breathtaking, but the height is dizzying. This transition, filled with potential and peril, is a rite of passage for which many find themselves unprepared. It's a moment that promises growth but demands courage. This book is your guide through that rite of passage. It's designed to equip you with the tools not just to survive but to thrive as a leader, whether you're taking the helm for the first time or seeking to refine your existing skills.

The heart of this book beats with a clear, unwavering purpose: to provide you with practical, actionable strategies that will enhance your leadership skills. It's a guide for everyone, crafted to meet you wherever you are on your leadership journey. Whether you have years of experience or are stepping into a leadership role for the first time without prior training, this book is for you.

Our vision is straightforward yet ambitious. We aim to transform leadership theory into tangible practice, enabling you to lead with confidence, empathy, and impact. Acquiring knowledge isn't enough; solid leadership is about turning that knowledge into action. We're here to show you how effective leadership can be learned, practiced, and perfected.

This book is specifically tailored for any adult embarking on leadership roles or aiming to elevate their leadership game. The guidance within these pages transcends industry boundaries, offering universal insights that are applicable in a myriad of scenarios. We've distilled years of research and real-world experience into an engaging, accessible, and, above all, actionable narrative.

As we journey through these chapters together, consider this book a conversation with a mentor who has walked this path before. I'll share stories, insights, and exercises designed to challenge and inspire you. By the end of our journey, you'll have a clearer understanding of what effective leadership looks like and a toolkit of strategies ready to be implemented.

Consider this book not just as a source of information but as a catalyst for transformation. Engage with the exercises, reflect on the insights, and apply the strategies in your day-to-day leadership. The path to becoming an effective leader is both a challenge and a privilege. It demands your best and rewards you with the opportunity to bring out the best in others.

To conclude this introduction, let me share a thought that has guided many leaders through their journeys: "Great leaders don't set out to be leaders … they set out to make a difference. It's never about the role—always about the goal." Let this be your mantra as we embark on this journey together.

As we turn the page to the first chapter, we'll dive into understanding the foundational qualities of effective leadership, setting the stage for the practical insights and transformational strategies that await. Let's begin this journey with an open mind and heart, ready to embrace the challenges and opportunities that effective leadership presents.

1

THE SPECTRUM OF LEADERSHIP STYLES—IDENTIFYING YOURS

As a leader, understanding oneself is as crucial as understanding those one leads. A leader's effectiveness is often mirrored in the performance and satisfaction of their team, making the exploration of leadership styles not just an academic exercise but a practical necessity. Leadership, in its essence, is the art of influencing others, and how a leader chooses to exert this influence can vary dramatically from one individual to another. This chapter delves into the spectrum of leadership styles, offering insights into identifying your style and its implications for team dynamics.

In the landscape of leadership, variety reigns supreme. Just as a gardener selects the right tools for different tasks in the garden, a leader must choose the most effective style for various situations and teams. The primary leadership styles—authoritative, democratic, and laissez-faire—serve as the foundational palette from which a leader paints their unique approach.

Diversity of Styles

The authoritative style is characterized by clear directives and a strong vision, with the leader at the helm setting directions and expecting the team to follow. It's similar to a seasoned captain navigating a ship through turbulent waters, where decisive action and clear commands are paramount. On the other hand, the democratic style thrives on collaboration. Here, the leader acts more like an orchestra conductor, valuing each musician's input to create a symphony. Lastly, the laissez-faire approach offers autonomy, allowing team members to innovate and make decisions, much like a mentor who provides guidance when needed but trusts in the individual's ability to learn and grow.

Each style has its place and utility, depending on the task at hand, the team's maturity, and the organizational culture. The leader's task is to understand and adeptly switch between these styles as circumstances require.

Self-Assessment

Identifying one's predominant leadership style requires introspection and, often, feedback from others. Tools and methods for this self-assessment range from formal instruments, like the Leadership Styles Assessment Tool, to informal feedback sessions with peers and team members. Reflecting on past leadership experiences can also offer valuable insights. Questions such as "How have I handled conflict?" or "What has been my approach to decision-making?" can illuminate patterns indicative of a particular style.

Impact on Teams

The influence of a leader's style on a team cannot be understated. An authoritative leader might accelerate decision-making and clarify goals but could also stifle creativity if not moderated. A democratic leader might boost morale and foster innovation through inclusive practices but could face challenges with swift decision-making. Meanwhile, a laissez-faire leader might empower individuals and encourage autonomy, yet risk a lack of direction if not careful. The key lies in understanding the needs of the team and the objectives to be achieved and then adapting the leadership style accordingly.

Flexibility and Application

Flexibility in leadership is like a skilled chef mastering the art of balancing flavors. Just as a dish might need a pinch of salt or a dash of vinegar to achieve the perfect taste, a situation might call for a shift in leadership style to address the team's needs effectively. This adaptability is not about changing one's core values or mimicking others but recognizing that different situations and team dynamics require different approaches.

For instance, consider a scenario where a new project is launched. An authoritative approach might be necessary to set the vision and direction in the initial stages. As the project progresses and team members become more familiar with their roles, shifting to a democratic style could help harness the team's collective creativity and expertise. As the project nears completion, adopting a laissez-faire approach might empower team members to take ownership and bring the project across the finish line.

This nuanced understanding and application of leadership styles underscore the importance of self-awareness and responsiveness to the ever-changing dynamics within teams and organizations. It's not merely about having a preferred style but about consciously choosing the most effective style for the situation at hand.

1.1 THE IMPACT OF EMOTIONAL INTELLIGENCE ON YOUR LEADERSHIP

In leadership, emotional intelligence (EQ) has emerged as a cornerstone for effective management and inspiring leadership. Unlike the traditional IQ, which measures rational intelligence, EQ focuses on one's ability to positively understand, use, and manage emotions to relieve stress, communicate effectively, empathize with others, overcome challenges, and defuse conflict. This ability is paramount in leadership roles, where the dynamics of human interactions are complex and varied.

Definition and Importance

Emotional intelligence refers to the capacity to be aware of, control, and express one's emotions and to handle interpersonal relationships judiciously and empathetically. In leadership, this translates to more than just managing teams efficiently; it means inspiring and motivating them, fostering a positive work environment, and navigating the intricate web of workplace relationships with finesse. A leader with high EQ can recognize their own emotional state and those of others, using this awareness to guide thinking, behavior, and decision-making.

Components of EQ

Breaking down the components of EQ, we find five key areas critical to its application in leadership:

- Self-awareness: Recognizing one's own emotions, strengths, weaknesses, values, and drivers and understanding their impact on others.
- Self-regulation: The ability to control or redirect disruptive emotions and impulses and adapt to changing circumstances.
- Motivation: A passion to work for reasons beyond money or status, a propensity to pursue goals with energy and persistence.
- Empathy: The ability to understand the emotional makeup of other people and treat them according to their emotional reactions.
- Social skills: Proficiency in managing relationships and building networks, as well as finding common ground and building rapport.

Each component plays a vital role in leadership, influencing everything from decision-making to team dynamics. For example, self-awareness allows leaders to recognize their biases and limitations, self-regulation helps them stay calm under pressure, motivation drives them to set and achieve goals, empathy enables them to understand and support their team, and social skills facilitate effective communication and conflict resolution.

Improving EQ

Enhancing one's EQ begins with a commitment to personal growth and a willingness to step out of one's comfort zone. Here are practical strategies and exercises for each component:

- For self-awareness, journal your emotional reactions and the situations that trigger them. Reflect on these entries to understand patterns in your behavior.

- To improve self-regulation, practice mindfulness and stress-reduction techniques. When faced with high-pressure situations, take a moment to breathe deeply and center yourself before responding.
- Boost motivation by setting personal and professional goals that align with your values. Break these down into smaller, achievable steps and celebrate your progress along the way.
- Develop empathy by actively listening to others. Try to understand their perspective without judgment and respond with compassion and understanding.
- Enhance social skills through active engagement. Volunteer for leadership roles in group settings, practice active listening and seek feedback on your communication and conflict-resolution techniques.

Real-World Impact

The positive effects of high EQ in leadership are well-documented. Consider a manager leading a team through a period of significant change. An emotionally intelligent leader would recognize their own anxiety about the change and manage it effectively, preventing it from influencing their interactions with the team. They would motivate the team by framing the change as an opportunity for growth, using empathy to understand and address team members' concerns, and employing social skills to communicate effectively and build consensus.

Another example might be a leader navigating a conflict between team members. An emotionally intelligent approach would involve recognizing the emotions at play, including the leader's own, and using empathetic listening to understand each team member's perspective. The leader could then use their social skills to facilitate a dialogue that allows each person to express their feelings and concerns, leading to a resolution that respects everyone's needs.

These examples underscore how emotional intelligence can transform challenges into growth and development opportunities for leaders and their teams. By focusing on developing EQ, leaders can build stronger relationships, foster a positive work environment, and navigate the complexities of organizational life with greater ease and effectiveness.

1.2 ADAPTING YOUR LEADERSHIP STYLE TO TEAM NEEDS

In the dynamic world of leadership, the ability to adjust your approach based on the unique needs of your team stands out as a critical skill. More is needed to have a preferred style; effective leaders recognize when to pivot and adapt their style to foster team cohesion, drive performance, and achieve organizational goals. This section explores practical steps for assessing team needs, understanding situational leadership, navigating common challenges, and maintaining a mindset geared toward continuous improvement.

Assessing Team Needs

The first step in adapting your leadership style is deeply understanding your team's current landscape. This requires a methodical approach to uncovering the group's strengths, weaknesses, and overall dynamics.

Conduct individual and team assessments:

- Utilize tools like personality tests, skill assessments, and performance reviews to gather data about your team members. Additionally, team-wide assessments help identify collective strengths and areas for development.
- Hold one-on-one meetings: Engage in candid conversations with each team member. These discussions can provide insights into individual aspirations, concerns, and perceptions of the team's functioning.
- Observe team interactions: Pay close attention to how team members communicate and collaborate during meetings and on projects. Observation can reveal underlying team dynamics, including leadership, communication patterns, and conflict resolution strategies.
- Solicit feedback: Encourage team members to provide feedback on their needs, preferences, and perceptions of team dynamics. This can be done through surveys, suggestion boxes, or facilitated group discussions.

Situational Leadership

The concept of situational leadership, developed by Paul Hersey and Kenneth Blanchard, posits that there is no single "best" leadership style. Instead, effective leaders adapt their style based on the individual's or team's maturity level and the specific situation.

- Understand the four leadership styles: Situational leadership identifies four primary styles - directing, coaching, supporting, and delegating. Each style corresponds to different levels of team maturity and readiness.

- Evaluate team maturity: Assess your team's maturity level, considering factors such as skill level, confidence, motivation, and willingness to take responsibility.
- Match your style to team needs: Adjust your leadership approach based on the team's maturity. For instance, a new team may require a more directive approach, while a highly skilled and motivated team might benefit from a delegating style.

Overcoming Challenges

Adapting your leadership style to meet team needs is not without its challenges. Here are some strategies for navigating some common obstacles:

- Resistance to change: Some team members may resist changes in leadership style, especially if they are used to a particular approach. Address this by clearly communicating the reasons for the change and involving the team in the transition process.
- Misalignment with personal leadership preferences: You may find that your natural leadership style does not align with what your team needs. To overcome this, seek training and mentorship to develop flexibility in your leadership approach. Practice stepping out of your comfort zone and experimenting with different styles in low-risk situations.
- Difficulty in assessing team maturity accurately: Misjudging team maturity can lead to mismatches in leadership style. Enhance your assessment skills by seeking input from multiple sources, including team members, peers, and other leaders. Regularly revisit and reassess team maturity as your team evolves.

Continuous Improvement

Embracing a mindset of continuous learning and adaptation is vital for leaders looking to adjust their style effectively to team needs. This involves:

- Regular reflection and self-assessment: Set aside time to reflect on your leadership effectiveness regularly. Consider maintaining a leadership journal to record observations, challenges, successes, and areas for growth.
- Seek feedback: Actively seek feedback from your team and peers on your leadership style and its impact. Use this feedback to improve your leadership style.
- Invest in professional development: Participate in leadership development programs, workshops, and seminars focusing on building adaptable leadership skills. These opportunities can provide new insights and strategies for effectively leading diverse teams.
- Stay informed: Stay abreast of new research and developments in leadership. Reading books, attending conferences, and joining professional networks can provide fresh perspectives and ideas for adapting your leadership approach.

In summary, the ability to adapt your leadership style to meet your team's evolving needs is a hallmark of effective leadership. By assessing team needs, employing situational leadership, navigating common challenges, and committing to continuous improvement, you can create a dynamic and responsive leadership approach that drives team success and fosters a positive, productive work environment.

1.3 AUTHENTICITY IN LEADERSHIP: BEING TRUE TO YOUR STYLE

Authenticity acts as the thread that binds trust and respect together, creating a strong, resilient fabric. When leaders present their true selves, their teams are more likely to rally behind them, fostering an environment of mutual respect and open communication. Authenticity in leadership is not about revealing every personal detail or disregarding professionalism; it's about being genuine in intentions, actions, and how one interacts with others.

The Value of Authenticity

Authenticity is the bedrock upon which trust is built. People gravitate towards genuine and transparent leaders, as this authenticity makes them more approachable and relatable. It's easier to trust someone when you feel they're being honest about who they are and what they stand for. Moreover, authentic leaders inspire their teams to be genuine, creating a culture of openness and honesty that can drive collective success.

Finding Your Authentic Style

Discovering and refining one's authentic leadership style is a process that requires introspection and feedback. Here are some steps to guide you through this journey:

- Reflect on your values and beliefs: Your leadership style should be an extension of your core values and beliefs. Reflect on what matters most to you and how these principles can guide your leadership.
- Gather feedback: Ask colleagues, mentors, and team members for feedback on your leadership approach. Pay

attention to patterns that may indicate how your authenticity (or lack thereof) is perceived.

- Identify role models: Think of leaders you admire and analyze what aspects of their leadership style resonate with you. Consider how their authenticity influences their leadership and how you can incorporate similar traits into your own style.
- Experiment with different approaches: Leadership is not one-size-fits-all. Experiment with different approaches and observe what feels most natural to you and what garners positive responses from your team.

Challenges to Authenticity

While striving to be an authentic leader, you may face several challenges. Recognizing these hurdles and knowing how to overcome them can help you maintain your authenticity:

- Pressure to conform: Organizational cultures or societal expectations can pressure leaders to conform to a certain mold. To overcome this, remain steadfast in your values and beliefs and seek out environments or roles that align with your authentic self.
- Fear of vulnerability: Sharing personal stories or admitting mistakes can make leaders feel vulnerable. However, vulnerability can be a strength. It humanizes you and can deepen connections between you and your team. Start with small disclosures and gradually increase as you become more comfortable.
- Balancing professionalism with authenticity: Finding the right balance between professionalism and authenticity can be tricky. Focus on being genuine in your intentions

and transparent in your communications while maintaining the decorum expected in your role.

- Evolving as a leader: As you grow and develop, so will your authentic leadership style. This evolution can sometimes lead to a perceived lack of consistency, but regular reflection and communication about your growth process can help mitigate this perception.

Consistency

Consistency in your actions, decisions, and interactions underpins the credibility of your authenticity. It reassures your team that you are reliable and that your leadership is grounded in a stable set of values and principles. Consistency doesn't mean you're inflexible or unchanging; rather, it signifies that even as you adapt and evolve, the core of who you are remains constant. Here are ways to maintain consistency:

- Set clear expectations: Clearly communicate your values, leadership philosophy, and expectations to your team. This clarity helps prevent misunderstandings and ensures everyone is on the same page.
- Practice what you preach: Align your actions with your words. If you advocate for open communication, ensure you're approachable and willing to listen to your team's ideas and concerns.
- Be accountable: Take responsibility for your decisions and actions. When mistakes happen, admit them and use them as learning opportunities. This reinforces your authenticity and models responsible behavior for your team.
- Stay grounded in your values: Regularly revisit your values and ensure your leadership practices reflect them. This

internal compass will guide your decisions and actions, helping you maintain consistency even in the face of challenges.

Maintaining authenticity in leadership is an ongoing process that demands self-awareness, courage, and a commitment to personal growth. It's about showing up as your true self, day in and day out, and leading in a way that is congruent with your values and beliefs. This approach engenders trust and respect and inspires those around you to be their best selves. As you continue to refine your authentic leadership style, remember that the most impactful leaders are not those who try to fit a particular mold but those who lead with sincerity, integrity, and a genuine concern for their team.

2

TRANSITIONING FROM PEER TO LEADER

Imagine stepping onto a stage only to find that the script you had memorized has changed overnight. Yesterday, you were part of the ensemble, blending your voice with others. Today, you're expected to lead the chorus, hitting the right notes to guide the entire performance. This shift from peer to leader is profound, requiring a nuanced understanding of not just the role but also the relationships that define it. Here, we navigate the delicate dance of asserting your new role with respect, maintaining friendships while stepping into authority, and laying down the groundwork for a leadership style that's both effective and respected.

2.1 STRATEGIES FOR ASSERTING YOUR NEW ROLE RESPECTFULLY

Setting Boundaries

Clear boundaries are the framework within which productive, respectful relationships can flourish. Think of them as the guidelines on a playground; they don't limit the fun, they ensure it. When you move into a leadership role, redefining these lines with your now-former peers becomes crucial. This isn't about creating distance but about fostering mutual respect. For instance, if you used to join the team for after-work drinks every Friday, you might now choose to do this less frequently, signaling your new role while still maintaining those important connections.

Communicating Changes

Effective communication is the bedrock of this transition. It's not just about announcing your new title in a team meeting; it's about sharing your vision, how you see roles evolving (including your own), and setting clear expectations. A practical step here is to schedule individual meetings with team members. Use this time not just to outline the changes but to listen. Understand their concerns, expectations, and how they see their place in this new chapter. It's about paving a two-way street right from the start.

Balancing Friendships and Leadership

The leap from colleague to superior doesn't mean you have to forsake friendships. It means learning to navigate them with a new map. Transparency and honesty are your best tools here. Sit down with your friends on the team and talk about your new role. Discuss how things might change and how they might stay the same. It's about finding that balance where you can still share a joke or a coffee, but when it comes to work, there's a clear understanding of your role as their leader. Remember, respect is a two-way street.

Early Wins

Gaining respect and establishing credibility can begin with what are known as "early wins"—those achievable goals that can be quickly met to gain team confidence. Identify a couple of low-hanging fruits—tasks or projects that you know your team can excel at— and tackle these first. Celebrate these successes together, highlighting the collective effort and individual contributions. This boosts morale and cements your leadership capabilities to guide the team to success.

In summary, transitioning from a peer to a leader is a nuanced process that demands clear communication, the redefinition of relationships, and strategic actions to establish your leadership effectively. It's about striking the right balance between maintaining genuine connections and asserting your new role with the authority it demands. This chapter provides practical steps to navigate this transition smoothly, ensuring you lead with confidence and the respect of your team.

2.2 BUILDING CREDIBILITY AS A NEW LEADER

Navigating the shift from peer to leader not only demands a reevaluation of interpersonal dynamics but also necessitates the establishment of credibility. Credibility, once solidified, acts as the foundation upon which effective leadership is constructed. It's the currency that enables leaders to motivate, inspire, and guide their teams toward shared objectives. The process of building this essential asset involves consistent leadership practices, fostering open communication, demonstrating competence, and actively soliciting feedback.

Consistent Leadership Practices

The essence of credibility lies in predictability. When your team knows what to expect from you, trust grows. This trust is cultivated through actions and decisions that are anchored in consistency. For instance, if you commit to weekly check-ins, ensure they occur without fail. Similarly, uphold the same standards for all team members, including yourself, regarding performance evaluations or adherence to deadlines. Such predictability in your leadership behavior not only fosters a sense of security among your team members but also sets a clear standard for what is expected, thereby reinforcing your role as a leader who is both fair and reliable.

Open Communication

The cornerstone of any strong relationship is open, honest communication, and the rapport between a leader and their team is no exception. It is crucial to create an environment where team members feel comfortable sharing their thoughts, concerns, and ideas without fear of judgment or reprisal. This can be facilitated through regular team meetings and one-on-one sessions where dialogue is encouraged and every voice is heard. Moreover, transparency about decision-making processes, strategy changes, or organizational goal shifts demystifies leadership actions. It helps team members understand the 'why' behind your decisions, further solidifying your standing as a credible leader.

Demonstrating Competence

While stepping into a leadership role, showcasing your expertise and competence in both your domain and leadership abilities is vital. This doesn't mean you need to have all the answers, but being resourceful and knowledgeable about where to find them is key. For example, you might need to learn the best way to navigate a particular client request, but you can demonstrate competence by consulting with more experienced colleagues or researching best practices. Additionally, staying abreast of industry trends and continuously seeking to enhance your skill set shows your commitment to your role and sets a positive example for your team.

Soliciting Feedback

A leader's growth is an ongoing process, significantly enriched by constructive feedback. Actively seeking input from your team on your leadership style, decision-making, and overall team dynamics is invaluable. This can be achieved through anonymous surveys, feedback forms, or designated feedback sessions. Importantly, it's not just about collecting feedback but acting on it. When your team sees their suggestions being implemented or at least considered, it reinforces your credibility as a leader who values their input and is committed to mutual growth and improvement.

In the journey to build credibility as a new leader, the emphasis lies in demonstrating through actions that you are consistent, communicative, competent, and open to feedback. These elements, woven together, form the fabric of a leadership style that is not only respected but also effective in fostering a motivated, cohesive, and high-performing team.

2.3 HANDLING RESENTMENT AND RESISTANCE

Moving into a leadership role often means sailing into the wind of resistance and resentment. These are natural human reactions, especially in environments where yesterday's peers become today's reports. Understanding the undercurrents that cause these feelings and addressing them with empathy and strategic communication can transform potential obstacles into opportunities for team cohesion and growth.

Understanding the Roots

Resentment and resistance don't spring up without reason. They are often rooted in fears of change, perceived injustices, or concerns about altered dynamics. For instance, a team member might fear their contributions will be undervalued under new leadership, or there may be underlying concerns about favoritism. Identifying these causes requires a leader to look beyond surface-level expressions of dissatisfaction, seeking to understand the deeper concerns at play.

- Fear of Change: Many resist new leadership because they are uncertain how changes will impact their roles, responsibilities, or the team's culture.
- Perceived Injustices: Some team members might feel injustice or bias if the promotion process isn't transparent.
- Altered Dynamics: Concerns about how relationships will change with a peer becoming a leader can also lead to resistance.

Empathy and Listening

Empathy is the bridge that connects leadership intentions with team perceptions. Showing genuine concern for team members' feelings and viewpoints opens the door to trust and mutual respect. Active listening is critical in this process, allowing leaders to understand the emotions and motivations behind resistance.

- Active Listening Sessions: Schedule sessions dedicated to listening to team members' concerns without immediately trying to provide solutions. This demonstrates respect for their viewpoints.
- Empathetic Responses: Respond to concerns with empathy, acknowledging the emotions involved and validating feelings before moving towards solutions.

Navigating Difficult Conversations

Difficult conversations are inevitable in leadership, especially when addressing resentment and resistance. Approaching these discussions with a plan can lead to productive outcomes.

- Prepare Mentally and Emotionally: Before the conversation, take time to prepare mentally. Reflect on the main points you need to address and your goals for the outcome.
- Create a Safe Environment: Ensure the conversation occurs in a private, neutral setting where both parties feel safe to express themselves. Start the discussion by affirming your commitment to a positive working relationship.
- Use "I" Statements: To avoid placing blame or making the other person defensive, frame your observations and

feelings with "I" statements, such as "I've noticed ..." or "I feel ..."

- Seek to Understand, Then to Be Understood: Listen to the other person's perspective fully before sharing your own. This demonstrates respect and openness to dialogue.
- Agree on Actionable Steps: End the conversation with agreed-upon steps to address the concerns raised. This could involve regular check-ins, specific changes in workflows, or other actions that address the root causes of resentment.

Building Support

Transforming resistance into support doesn't happen overnight. It requires consistent effort and strategic engagement with your team to build a foundation of trust and respect.

- Demonstrate Equity: Through your actions, show that each team member is valued equally. Make decisions based on fairness and merit, and be transparent about how and why decisions are made.
- Engage in Team Building: Organize activities that foster team cohesion and allow you to participate as a team member, not just its leader. This can help break down barriers and build camaraderie.
- Provide Opportunities for Input: Regularly solicit input from team members on decisions that affect them. This fosters a sense of ownership and demonstrates that you value their contributions.
- Recognize and Reward Contributions: Make it a point to recognize and reward team members' efforts and achievements publicly. This boosts morale and shows you are attentive and appreciative of their hard work.

Handling resentment and resistance as a new leader is a delicate balancing act. It requires a deep understanding of the underlying causes, a commitment to empathetic listening, skillful navigation of difficult conversations, and strategic actions to build support. By addressing these challenges head-on, with sensitivity and fairness, you can lay the groundwork for a strong, cohesive team that is aligned with your leadership vision and goals.

2.4 FOSTERING A CULTURE OF GROWTH AS A NEW LEADER

A mark of forward-thinking leadership is nurturing an environment that champions continuous improvement and learning. It's about more than just meeting quarterly targets; it's about setting your team on a path of perpetual growth and development. Here, we explore strategies for embedding a culture of growth within your team, emphasizing the leader's pivotal role in this transformative process.

Encouraging Continuous Learning

Creating a team that values and pursues learning requires a multifaceted approach. Start by integrating learning into the fabric of your team's daily routines. This could mean starting meetings with a "learning moment" where team members share insights from recent experiences or articles they've read. Additionally, making a diverse range of learning resources readily available and accessible is key. Consider creating a shared digital library of courses, webinars, and books relevant to your team's field.

Encourage participation in industry conferences and workshops, not just as attendees but as contributors or speakers. This enhances learning and positions your team as thought leaders in your industry. To reinforce this learning culture, consider setting aside a dedicated "learning hour" each week where team members can focus on personal development activities without the pressure of immediate work tasks.

Modeling Growth

As a leader, your attitude towards growth and learning sets the tone for your team. Demonstrating a commitment to your own development is as critical as encouraging your team to pursue their growth. Share your learning experiences, both the successes and the challenges, openly with your team. This might include discussing a new management technique you're experimenting with or a recent course you completed.

Your willingness to show vulnerability in your learning process can significantly lower your team's barriers to embracing new challenges. It's also beneficial to visibly apply the insights you've gained from your learning experiences to your leadership practices. This not only reinforces the value of continuous learning but also demonstrates its practical impact.

Creating Opportunities for Development

Beyond encouraging learning, actively creating opportunities for development within the team is vital. One practical approach is to tailor development opportunities to individual team members' career aspirations and strengths. This personalized approach ensures that development activities are both relevant and engaging.

Implementing a mentorship program within your team can facilitate personalized development while also strengthening team bonds. Pairing less experienced team members with more seasoned colleagues allows for the transfer of knowledge and skills in a supportive one-on-one setting.

Another strategy is to rotate team members through different roles or projects. This exposes them to new challenges and areas of the business, broadening their skill sets and perspectives. It's important to frame these rotations as growth opportunities and provide the necessary support to ensure team members feel equipped to take on these new challenges.

Recognizing and Rewarding Growth

Acknowledging and celebrating growth and achievements is crucial for sustaining motivation and reinforcing a culture of development. Regular recognition can take many forms, from public acknowledgment in team meetings to personalized notes of appreciation.

Consider implementing a "growth spotlight" in your team newsletters or meetings, where you highlight specific examples of team members' development achievements. This will not only celebrate individual accomplishments but also inspire the entire team.

In addition to recognition, providing tangible rewards for significant learning achievements can further incentivize continuous development. These rewards might include additional professional development funds, opportunities to lead new projects, or even promotions.

Your leadership is instrumental in enhancing your team's growth culture. By advocating for continuous learning, embodying a growth mindset, generating development opportunities, and celebrating progress, you lay the groundwork for a team that not only achieves its current goals but is also poised for future challenges.

As we wrap up this exploration of fostering a growth culture, we can see that the role of a leader extends beyond managing tasks and meeting objectives. It's about inspiring your team to see beyond the horizon, constantly seek improvement, and enthusiastically pursue learning. This commitment not only elevates the individual team members but also propels the entire team toward sustained success and innovation.

Moving forward, we will delve into the practicalities of building and maintaining a high-performing team, focusing on the strategies and leadership practices that drive team effectiveness and resilience.

3

EFFECTIVE COMMUNICATION— THE BACKBONE OF LEADERSHIP

Imagine standing before a large mural, its vast canvas stretching out before you filled with a complex mesh of colors, shapes, and textures. Your task as a leader is not unlike being the artist of such a mural, where every brush stroke—every word you utter, every message you craft—adds to the picture your team sees and understands. The clarity of this picture and its ability to inspire and move people toward action hinges on the effectiveness of your communication. This chapter is about refining those brushstrokes, ensuring that your messages reach your team and resonate with them, spurring them into action, and aligning them with your vision.

3.1 CRAFTING CLEAR AND INSPIRING MESSAGES

Precision and Clarity

The first step in ensuring your message is understood is to strip away any ambiguity. It's like giving someone directions; the more precise you are, the less likely they are to get lost. When communicating with your team, aim for simplicity and directness. Avoid jargon unless you're certain everyone understands it. If you're assigning tasks, be explicit about what needs to be done, by whom, and by when. This clarity not only minimizes confusion but also empowers your team to execute tasks with confidence.

A helpful exercise is to review your recent communications—emails, meeting notes, presentations—and assess them for clarity. Look for any assumptions you might have made about the reader's knowledge or any vague language that could be interpreted in multiple ways. Then, rewrite these communications carefully and notice their difference in response and execution.

Motivational Language

Words have the power to inspire. They can galvanize a team into action, ignite a passion for a project, or instill a sense of urgency. Incorporating motivational language into your communications can transform mundane tasks into exciting challenges. When setting goals or assigning tasks, frame them in a way that highlights their importance to the team and the organization. Use positive affirmations and acknowledge your team's capability to meet and exceed expectations.

For instance, instead of saying, "I need this report by Friday," try, "Your expertise can make this report shine, and having it by Friday will help us stay ahead of schedule." This slight shift motivates and shows trust in your team's abilities.

Aligning Message with Vision

Every communication should be a building block in the structure of your team's understanding of your vision. Effective communication involves connecting the dots between daily tasks and the bigger picture, ensuring everyone understands how their work contributes to the organization's goals.

Start meetings by reminding the team of its objectives and ending them by linking the discussion back to those objectives. When assigning new projects, explain how they fit into the team's overarching goals. This alignment not only helps maintain focus but also fosters a sense of purpose and belonging among team members.

Medium Matters

How you convey your message can be as important as the message itself. Different mediums have different impacts. An email might be sufficient for sharing information, but a face-to-face meeting (or video call, if remote work is involved) might be better for discussing sensitive issues or brainstorming sessions where collaboration is key.

Consider the content of your message and the context in which it's being delivered to choose the most effective medium. For urgent matters, a direct phone call might be the best choice. A detailed email might be more appropriate for complex information that needs to be referred back to. And in-person meetings can be invaluable for fostering team spirit or discussing values and vision.

To implement this, create a communication plan outlining what messages are best suited for each medium. This could include guidelines on when to use email versus a meeting, how to decide between a phone call and a direct message, and what information is best conveyed in written form.

Effective communication is the backbone of successful leadership. It's about ensuring your message is heard, understood, and embraced. Focusing on precision and clarity, using motivational language, aligning your messages with your vision, and choosing the right medium can elevate your communication from mere information transmission to a powerful leadership tool.

3.2 ACTIVE LISTENING: A LEADER'S SUPERPOWER

Often overlooked in the toolkit of leadership skills, active listening is one of the most powerful. Active listening is about more than just hearing words but fully understanding the message being conveyed. Here, we break down the essentials of active listening and how it can transform your leadership.

Fundamentals of Active Listening

Active listening involves several key components that work together to ensure comprehension and convey respect and empathy to the speaker.

- Non-Verbal Cues: Much of communication is non-verbal. As a leader, your body language should communicate attentiveness and openness. This means maintaining eye contact, nodding to show understanding, and using facial expressions that match the conversation's tone. These cues encourage the speaker and signal that you are fully engaged.
- Paraphrasing: To demonstrate understanding, it's effective to paraphrase what's been said. This doesn't mean repeating their words verbatim but summarizing the main points in your own words. This clarifies that you've grasped the essence of their message and allows any misinterpretations to be corrected.

Creating a Listening Environment

An environment conducive to active listening is one where team members feel safe and valued. Achieving this requires intentional actions and settings.

- Physical Space: Opt for settings that are private and free from interruptions for sensitive or in-depth discussions. Even in open-office environments, finding a quiet corner can make a difference.
- Open Door Policy: Cultivate a culture where your team members know they can approach you with their ideas, concerns, and feedback. This policy, however, should be more than just a metaphorical open door; it should be an evident practice where team members see their input welcomed and valued.
- Scheduled One-on-One: Regularly scheduled meetings with team members provide dedicated listening time. These should be seen not as status updates but as opportunities to understand their challenges, aspirations, and feedback on the team's direction.

Overcoming Listening Barriers

Several barriers can hinder effective listening. Identifying and addressing these can significantly enhance your ability to listen actively.

- Preconceptions and Bias: We all carry biases that can color our perception of what's being said. Challenge yourself to listen without judgment, focusing on understanding the speaker's perspective, regardless of your opinions about the topic or the person.

- Distractions: In our always-connected world, distractions are constant. Make a conscious effort to minimize them by silencing notifications, closing unnecessary tabs, or even stepping away from your desk to give the speaker your undivided attention.
- Interrupting: It's natural to want to offer solutions or opinions, but interrupting can convey that you value your input more than understanding theirs. Practice patience, allowing the speaker to express their thoughts fully before responding.

Listening to Understand, Not to Respond

The ultimate goal of active listening is to comprehend the speaker's message, not just formulate your response. This shift in focus requires a deliberate effort to stay present in the conversation.

- Pause Before Responding: After the speaker finishes, take a moment to digest what's been said. This pause is respectful and gives you time to formulate a thoughtful response.
- Ask Open-Ended Questions: Encourage deeper exploration of the topic by asking questions that require more than a yes/no answer. Questions like "Can you tell me more about that?" or "How did that make you feel?" prompt further sharing and show genuine interest.

Active listening is more than a skill; it demonstrates respect and a foundation for trust. By fully engaging with your team members, acknowledging their perspectives, and responding with empathy and understanding, you reinforce your commitment to their success and well-being. This approach not only enhances team communication but also deepens your relationships, creating a more cohesive and motivated team.

3.3 FEEDBACK LOOPS: ENCOURAGING OPEN DIALOGUE

Creating a culture where feedback flows freely and constructively is much like laying down the irrigation system for a garden. Just as the right channels ensure water reaches every plant, effectively structured feedback loops ensure insights and observations circulate, nurturing growth throughout your team. This section outlines establishing feedback loops that foster transparency and continuous improvement.

Constructing Effective Feedback Loops

To cultivate a robust feedback environment, start by laying the foundational structures that facilitate ongoing dialogue. Begin with setting a clear purpose for the feedback—whether it's for improving processes, enhancing performance, or fostering personal development. Next, integrate feedback mechanisms into the regular rhythm of your team's activities. This could be through structured sessions at the end of projects, regular one-on-ones, or digital platforms allowing anonymous feedback.

- Scheduled Feedback Sessions: Introduce regular, scheduled opportunities for feedback, such as monthly review meetings or weekly check-ins, ensuring they're seen as a standard part of your team's operations.
- Anonymous Channels: Sometimes, team members may feel more comfortable providing feedback anonymously, especially if it's critical. Tools and platforms allowing anonymous feedback can be valuable in these instances.
- 360-Degree Feedback: Implement a 360-degree feedback process that allows everyone to receive feedback from their peers, subordinates, and superiors. This

comprehensive view encourages a culture of transparency and mutual respect.

Encouraging Participation

In many teams, the challenge isn't just collecting feedback but encouraging active participation in the feedback process. To engage your team:

- Lead by Example: Show your team that you value feedback by actively seeking it out for yourself and responding positively. Your openness to feedback sets the tone for the entire team.
- Normalize Feedback: Make giving and receiving feedback regular parts of team interactions by regularly discussing the value of feedback and sharing examples of how it has led to positive changes.
- Provide Training: Offer training sessions on constructively giving and receiving feedback. This can help alleviate anxiety around feedback by equipping team members with the skills to navigate these conversations effectively.

Handling Negative Feedback

Receiving negative feedback can be challenging, yet it's a vital part of personal and team development. When faced with critical feedback:

- Stay Calm and Open: Initially, you might feel defensive, but listening openly to what's being said is crucial. Taking a moment to breathe and center yourself can help maintain composure.

- Seek Understanding: Before responding, ask questions to clarify the feedback and ensure you fully understand the raised concerns. This shows that you're taking the feedback seriously and helps prevent misunderstandings.
- Thank and Reflect: Always thank the person for their feedback, regardless of its nature. Then, take time to reflect on the input privately, considering how it aligns with your own observations and what changes it may necessitate.

Actionable Insights

The true power of feedback lies in its ability to drive action. Transforming feedback into actionable insights involves several steps:

- Identify Themes: Look for common themes or patterns in the feedback you receive. These can highlight areas that need attention, whether it's a specific skill, a process within the team, or how decisions are communicated.
- Develop an Action Plan: For each major theme identified, develop a plan that outlines specific steps to address the issue. Assign clear responsibilities and timelines to ensure accountability.
- Follow-up: Regularly review the progress of your action plans with your team. This will keep the plans on track and show your team that their feedback leads to tangible changes.
- Share Learnings: When feedback leads to a positive outcome, share this with your team. Highlighting how feedback has been instrumental in driving improvements reinforces the value of the feedback process.

Incorporating effective feedback loops into your team's culture is not a one-time task but an ongoing effort. It requires commitment, openness, and a genuine desire for continuous improvement. By establishing clear structures for feedback, encouraging active participation, handling negative feedback constructively, and turning insights into action, you lay the groundwork for a team that communicates openly and thrives on mutual support and continuous growth.

3.4 NAVIGATING DIFFICULT CONVERSATIONS WITH GRACE

Facing challenging discussions is inevitable in leadership. Whether it's addressing performance issues, mediating conflicts, or delivering unwelcome news, the manner in which these conversations are handled can significantly impact team morale and trust. A thoughtful approach to these dialogues can turn potential conflicts into moments of growth and understanding.

Preparation and Mindset

Entering difficult conversations requires thoughtful preparation and setting the right intentions from the outset. Begin by clarifying your objectives for the conversation. What is the ideal outcome? How can you address the issue in a way that respects all parties involved? Equally important is adopting a mindset aimed at resolution and growth rather than blame or confrontation. Reflect on any personal biases or emotions that might color your perspective, and commit to maintaining an open and constructive attitude throughout the discussion.

- Outline the key points you must cover, keeping your language neutral and focused on behaviors rather than personal attributes.

- Anticipate potential responses and plan how you might address them calmly and constructively.
- Choose a setting that ensures privacy and minimizes interruptions, creating a space where open, honest communication can thrive.

Emotional Intelligence in Conversations

Leveraging emotional intelligence can significantly smooth the process of navigating through tough discussions. This involves being attuned to your own emotions and those of the person you're speaking with. Pay attention to non-verbal cues—such as body language and tone of voice—that may indicate how the other person feels. Responding to these cues with empathy can help de-escalate tension and foster a sense of mutual under-standing.

- Practice active listening, giving the other person space to express their thoughts and feelings without interruption.
- Acknowledge and validate their emotions, even if you disagree with their perspective. This can help bridge gaps in understanding and pave the way for constructive dialogue.
- Manage your own emotional responses, taking a moment to breathe and center yourself if the conversation becomes heated.

Framework for Difficult Conversations

A structured approach can make difficult conversations more manageable and productive. One effective framework involves three key stages: opening, exploring, and closing.

- Opening: Start by setting a positive, collaborative tone. Express your intention to resolve the issue to benefit everyone involved. Clearly state the topic of the conversation without assigning blame.
- Exploring: Use this stage to delve into the issue, encouraging open dialogue. Ask open-ended questions to gather information and perspectives. Share your own thoughts and feelings, using "I" statements to communicate your concerns without accusing or blaming.
- Closing: Aim to conclude the conversation with clear, agreed-upon steps for moving forward. This could involve setting specific goals, agreeing on behavioral changes, or planning follow-up meetings to assess progress. Ensure both parties leave the conversation clearly and understand what comes next.

Follow-up and Resolution

The true test of a difficult conversation's effectiveness lies in the follow-up. Demonstrating commitment to the agreed-upon actions reinforces trust and shows that the conversation was more than just talk.

- Schedule a follow-up meeting to review progress on the action items discussed. This keeps the momentum going and provides an opportunity for additional support or adjustments as needed.
- Recognize and celebrate improvements, no matter how small. Positive reinforcement can motivate continued progress and strengthen your relationship with your team members.
- If the situation doesn't improve, be prepared to take additional steps. This might involve revisiting the

conversation with new insights, considering alternative solutions, or, in some cases, escalating the matter according to organizational policies.

Tackling difficult conversations thoughtfully and respectfully is a hallmark of effective leadership. By preparing thoroughly, applying emotional intelligence, following a clear framework, and ensuring follow-up, you can turn challenging discussions into opportunities for growth and stronger connections within your team.

As we close this chapter, remember that the art of communication extends far beyond the words we speak. Our ability to listen, empathize, and engage with honesty and integrity is mirrored. The skills and strategies discussed here not only enhance our interactions but also strengthen the very fabric of our teams, fostering an environment where trust, respect, and mutual growth prevail. Looking ahead, we'll explore the dynamics of diverse and inclusive leadership, examining how embracing a broad spectrum of perspectives can drive innovation and success.

4

LEADING ACROSS CULTURES— THE POWER OF UNDERSTANDING

In the vast mosaic of today's workplace, each piece—each individual—brings a unique color, shape, and texture to the bigger picture. The beauty of this diversity is undeniable, but so is the complexity of weaving these distinct pieces together into a cohesive work of art. For leaders, the challenge isn't just in appreciating this diversity but in effectively communicating across their teams' various cultural backgrounds. This chapter delves into the nuances of cross-cultural communication, offering strategies for navigating this rich but potentially tricky landscape.

4.1 UNDERSTANDING CULTURAL DIFFERENCES IN COMMUNICATION

Cultural Communication Norms

At the heart of cross-cultural communication lies the understanding that each culture has its own set of norms and expectations regarding communication. For instance, in some cultures, directness is valued and seen as a sign of honesty and efficiency. In others, indirect communication is the norm, where preserving harmony and saving face take precedence over blunt truth. Recognizing these differences is the first step in avoiding misunderstandings that can lead to conflict or discomfort within your team.

Consider this: When you provide feedback to a team member from a culture that values indirect communication, framing your feedback directly might cause unintended offense or discomfort, even if your intentions are positive. Conversely, being too indirect with someone from a culture that values directness might lead them to miss your point entirely.

Cultural Intelligence

Cultural intelligence, or CQ, measures your ability to relate and work effectively across cultures. Developing high CQ involves four key components:

- Cultural awareness: Recognizing that differences exist without assigning value (better or worse, right or wrong) to those differences.
- Cultural knowledge: Learning about different cultures, their norms, values, and communication styles.
- Cultural skills: Practicing and applying your knowledge of different cultures to improve your interactions.
- Cultural empathy: The ability to empathize with individuals from different cultural backgrounds, understanding their perspectives and feelings.

Improving your CQ is not a one-time task but an ongoing process of learning, reflection, and adaptation. It involves actively seeking knowledge about different cultures, being mindful and observant in cross-cultural interactions, and constantly refining your approach based on your experiences.

Adapting Your Communication Style

Adapting your communication style to be more inclusive and effective across cultures requires both flexibility and intentionality. Here are a few strategies:

- Listen more than you speak: This gives you a better chance to pick up on the subtle nuances of cross-cultural communication.
- Ask open-ended questions: Encourage team members to express their thoughts and feelings in their own words.
- Use clear and simple language: Avoid idioms, slang, and complex vocabulary that non-native speakers might need help understanding.
- Be mindful of non-verbal cues: Remember that gestures, eye contact, and physical proximity can have different meanings in different cultures.

Case Studies

Let's consider a real-life example: A multinational corporation introduced a global leadership training program designed by its head office in the United States. Initially, the program struggled with engagement from its Asian subsidiaries. Feedback revealed that the training's highly interactive and participatory style, typical in American educational settings, was uncomfortable for participants from cultures where learning is often more passive and respectful silence is valued in the classroom. By adapting the program to include more structured guidance and allowing for written rather than spoken participation, engagement levels significantly improved.

Another example involves a Swedish company known for its flat organizational structure and informal communication style, expanding into Japan, where hierarchical structures and formal communication are the norms. The Swedish managers had to adapt their approach, adopting more formal titles and communication styles in interactions with their Japanese colleagues to show respect for the cultural norms and to foster a more comfortable working environment.

These case studies highlight the importance of understanding and adapting to cultural communication norms. By doing so, leaders can build stronger, more cohesive teams that leverage their diverse perspectives for greater creativity and innovation.

4.2 ADAPTING LEADERSHIP COMMUNICATION TO REMOTE TEAMS

The shift toward remote work has transformed team communication and leadership dynamics. While it offers the advantages of tapping into global talent and flexibility, it also introduces distinct challenges that require a nuanced approach from leaders. The essence of leading remote teams lies in understanding these challenges and innovatively leveraging technology to maintain connection and cohesion.

Challenges of Remote Communication

Remote teams often need help with hurdles not present in traditional office settings. The lack of face-to-face interaction can lead to feelings of isolation among team members, making it harder to foster a sense of belonging and team spirit. Misunderstandings can also arise more frequently without the immediate feedback loop of in-person conversations, where nonverbal cues play a significant role in communication. Additionally, time zone differences can complicate scheduling, making real-time communication difficult and potentially delaying project progress.

Leveraging Technology

To navigate these challenges, leaders must become adept at using technology not just as a tool for communication but also to create an immersive and engaging team environment.

- Video Conferencing: Platforms like Zoom and Microsoft Teams can simulate face-to-face interactions, making meetings more personal and effective. Encourage video use during meetings to help team members feel more connected.
- Collaboration Tools: Utilize tools such as Slack, Trello, or Asana to keep projects organized and maintain open lines of communication. These platforms can also host non-work-related channels or boards to support social interactions and team bonding.
- Digital Workspaces: Create an online hub where your team can find all the resources, documents, and tools they need in one place. This will streamline work processes and reduce the feeling of being overwhelmed by scattered information.
- Virtual Office Hours: Set regular hours where you're available for impromptu video calls or chats. This mimics the open-door policy of physical offices and encourages team members to reach out with questions or to catch up.

Building Connection and Cohesion

Creating a cohesive team culture when members are dispersed requires thoughtful strategies that go beyond regular work meetings.

- Regular Check-ins: Individual check-ins allow you to touch base with team members professionally and personally. These conversations can highlight potential issues early on and provide support where needed.
- Virtual Team Building: Organize regular virtual team-building activities that are not work-related. These activities can help bridge the physical gap and build rapport, from online games to virtual coffee breaks or book clubs.
- Recognition and Celebration: Make an effort to celebrate team achievements and milestones in a virtual setting. Recognizing individual contributions during team calls or via team communication platforms can boost morale and reinforce a culture of appreciation.

Frequency and Transparency

Communication frequency and transparency become even more critical in a remote setting. Striking the right balance ensures that team members are well-informed and engaged without feeling micromanaged.

- Regular Updates: Provide consistent updates on company news, project progress, and team achievements. This keeps everyone in the loop and reinforces a sense of shared purpose.

- Open Forums: Host monthly or quarterly Q&A sessions where team members can voice concerns, ask questions, and provide feedback. This open forum fosters transparency and shows that leadership values team input.
- Clear Expectations: Communicate clearly your expectations regarding work hours, availability, and communication preferences. Establishing these guidelines helps prevent misunderstandings and ensures smooth collaboration.

The challenge in leading remote teams isn't just overcoming the barriers of distance but turning this work mode into an opportunity to create a dynamic, inclusive, and high-performing team. By embracing technology, fostering connection and cohesion, and maintaining open and frequent communication, leaders can help their remote teams thrive in this new landscape.

4.3 BRIDGING GENERATIONAL GAPS IN COMMUNICATION

In workplaces today, we often find a tapestry of ages, each thread woven with unique experiences, expectations, and communication methods. From the silent generation and baby boomers to Generation X, millennials, and Generation Z, the workforce has never been more diverse in age. While a significant asset, this diversity brings challenges, particularly when it comes to communication. Understanding these generational differences and finding ways to bridge the gaps is crucial for leaders aiming to foster a harmonious and productive environment.

Understanding Generational Differences

Each generation brings its own values, communication styles, and work ethics, shaped by the socio-economic conditions, technological advancements, and cultural shifts they experienced growing up. For instance, baby boomers generally value stability and hard work and may prefer face-to-face communication. In contrast, millennials and Generation Z, having grown up in the digital age, are more comfortable with fast-paced, digital forms of communication and value flexibility and work-life balance. Recognizing these differences is the first step in addressing potential communication challenges within a multigenerational team.

- Silent Generation and Baby Boomers: Often prefer formal communication channels and value respect for authority and structure.
- Generation X: Values independence and directness and may favor email as a primary communication tool.
- Millennials (Generation Y): Prefers collaborative work environments, values feedback, and often leans toward quick digital communication methods like instant messaging.
- Generation Z: Highly digital natives, comfortable multitasking across platforms, and values authenticity and social responsibility.

Creating Multigenerational Engagement

The key to engaging a multigenerational team is leveraging each generation's unique strengths and preferences while fostering mutual respect and understanding. This can be achieved through:

- Tailored Communication: Adapt your communication style to meet the preferences of different generations. This might mean varying the mix of communication tools used within the team, from traditional meetings and emails to instant messaging apps and social media platforms.
- Inclusive Meetings: Structure meetings to ensure they cater to various preferences, mixing traditional presentations with interactive elements. Encouraging participation from all team members, regardless of their preferred communication style, ensures everyone feels heard and valued.
- Shared Goals: Focus on common objectives that transcend generational divides. Highlighting shared goals can help bridge differences by uniting team members around a common purpose.

Leveraging Diverse Perspectives

The mix of perspectives and experiences across generations can be a tremendous asset to teams, driving innovation and creative problem-solving. To fully leverage this diversity:

- Cross-Generational Teams: Create project teams that include members from different generations. This not only facilitates the sharing of diverse viewpoints but also allows team members to learn from each other's strengths.
- Open Forums for Idea Sharing: Implement regular sessions dedicated to sharing ideas and insights across the team. Encourage members from different generations to present on topics where they have expertise or a unique perspective. This fosters respect for the knowledge and experiences each generation brings to the table.

Mentoring and Reverse Mentoring

Mentoring programs that pair older and younger team members can facilitate personal and professional growth for both mentors and mentees. Reverse mentoring, where younger team members mentor their older counterparts, particularly in areas like technology and current trends, can be especially beneficial in breaking down stereotypes and fostering mutual respect.

- Setting Clear Objectives: For mentoring relationships to be successful, it's important to establish clear goals. Whether it's learning a new skill, gaining insights into different areas of the business, or developing leadership abilities, having a clear focus helps ensure both parties gain value from the experience.
- Training and Support: Provide training on how to build a successful mentoring relationship for both mentors and mentees. This might include guidance on setting goals, giving and receiving feedback, and navigating generational differences.
- Feedback Loop: Incorporate a feedback mechanism within the mentoring program to continuously improve its effectiveness. Regular check-ins with mentors and mentees can help identify what's working well and where adjustments may be needed.

In sum, bridging generational gaps in communication is not about diminishing the differences or changing the inherent values of each generation. It's about creating an environment where those differences are acknowledged, respected, and leveraged for the collective benefit of the team. Through tailored communication strategies, inclusive meetings, leveraging diverse perspectives, and implementing mentoring programs, leaders can foster a culture of collaboration, learning, and mutual respect across generations. This not only enhances team cohesion but also drives innovation and success in an increasingly complex and interconnected world.

4.4 CREATING INCLUSIVE SPACES FOR ALL VOICES

The essence of inclusivity lies in recognizing and actively celebrating the multitude of voices within a team. Inclusivity is about crafting spaces where every team member feels valued and heard regardless of rank, seniority, or background. This section explores practical strategies to enhance inclusivity in team interactions, highlighting the critical role leaders play in fostering an environment where diversity is acknowledged and celebrated for the richness it brings.

Inclusivity in Team Meetings

Team meetings, the heartbeat of organizational communication, present a prime opportunity to practice inclusivity. Ensuring that every voice is heard in these gatherings starts with intentional planning and facilitation:

- Structured Agenda with Open Slots: While having a structured agenda keeps the meeting on track, including open slots where any team member can bring up topics ensures that everyone has the opportunity to contribute.
- Round-Robin Technique: Implement a round-robin approach for specific agenda items, inviting each participant to share their thoughts. This method ensures that quieter members are given the space to voice their opinions.
- Digital Platforms for Anonymity: Utilize digital platforms that allow team members to submit questions or

comments anonymously before or during the meeting. This can help highlight voices that might feel uncomfortable speaking up in a group setting.

Encouraging Minority Voices

Creating an environment where minority voices are encouraged to participate requires leaders to be both advocates and allies:

- Spotlight Segments: Dedicate segments of team meetings or company-wide gatherings to spotlight team members from underrepresented groups, allowing them to share their experiences and insights or lead a discussion on a topic of their expertise.
- Mentorship Programs: Establish mentorship programs aimed at supporting the professional development of minority team members. Pairing them with senior leaders or peers can boost their confidence and visibility within the organization.
- Inclusive Language: Be mindful of using inclusive language that does not inadvertently exclude or marginalize. This includes using correct pronouns, avoiding gendered language when unnecessary, and being cautious with idioms or cultural references that may not be universally understood.

Addressing Unconscious Bias

Unconscious biases, those automatic judgments and behaviors that stem from deep-seated attitudes, can subtly influence team dynamics and decision-making. Leaders play a crucial role in identifying and mitigating these biases:

- Training and Awareness: Invest in unconscious bias training for yourself and your team. Awareness is the first step toward change, and such training can help uncover biases that may be affecting team interactions.
- Diverse Hiring Panels: Utilize diverse hiring panels to mitigate bias in recruitment and promotion processes. Having multiple perspectives can help counteract individual biases and lead to more equitable decision-making.
- Feedback Mechanisms: Implement clear mechanisms for team members to report instances where they feel bias has influenced decisions or behavior. Creating a safe and responsive process for addressing these concerns is critical for maintaining trust and respect.

Celebrating Diversity

Recognizing and celebrating the diversity within a team not only reinforces a culture of inclusivity but also enhances creativity, innovation, and engagement:

- Cultural Celebrations: Encourage the celebration of various cultural holidays and events within the team. This not only educates but also honors the diverse backgrounds of team members.
- Diversity Forums: Host forums or discussion groups focused on topics related to diversity and inclusion. These can be opportunities for learning, sharing personal experiences, and discussing ways the organization can continue to improve its inclusivity efforts.
- Recognition of Diverse Contributions: Actively recognize and highlight the diverse contributions of team members.

Whether through company-wide communications, awards, or acknowledgments in meetings, showing appreciation for a wide range of contributions reinforces the value of diversity.

Crafting inclusive spaces where all voices are heard and valued is not a passive endeavor but an active commitment to leadership that embraces and celebrates diversity. It's about creating an environment where every individual feels empowered to share their unique perspectives, knowing they will be met with respect and appreciation. Through thoughtful strategies that encourage participation, address biases, and celebrate diversity, leaders can foster a culture of inclusivity that not only enriches the team but also drives innovation and success.

As we conclude this exploration of inclusivity, it's clear that the strength of a team lies not just in the sum of its parts but in the depth of its diversity. By championing inclusivity in every facet of team dynamics, leaders can unlock the full potential of their teams, paving the way for a more vibrant, innovative, and cohesive future. Moving forward, the focus shifts to the practicalities of building and nurturing high-performing teams, where the principles of inclusivity, understanding, and communication continue to play pivotal roles.

5

ASSEMBLING YOUR DREAM TEAM

Imagine walking into a room filled with different instruments, each with its unique sound and role. Now, consider your task is to create harmony; you must decide which instruments to bring together, how they will interact, and what music they will play. This is what it's like to build a high-performing team: it's about understanding each person's unique strengths and how those can be woven together to create something remarkable.

In this part of our exploration, we focus on identifying and leveraging your team's diverse strengths. Recognizing your team member's individual talents and knowing how to assemble these talents strategically can transform your team's operations, enhance problem-solving capabilities, foster innovation, and drive unparalleled results.

5.1 IDENTIFYING AND LEVERAGING DIVERSE STRENGTHS

Diversity as a Strength

Diversity isn't just a buzzword; it's a critical component of team success. When discussing diversity in this context, we're looking beyond demographics. We're considering the variety of skills, experiences, thought processes, and problem-solving approaches each person brings to the team. Like a master chef expertly combining flavors to create a dish that's more delicious than the sum of its parts, a skilled leader can blend these diverse strengths to push the team toward excellence.

Consider a project that requires creative thinking, detailed planning, and effective execution. By identifying who on your team thrives in creative brainstorming, who can break down the project into manageable tasks, and who excels at keeping the team on track, you can delegate responsibilities that play to each member's strengths.

Assessment Tools and Techniques

To effectively leverage the strengths within your team, you first need to identify them. Various tools and techniques can help with this:

- StrengthsFinder: A popular assessment that helps individuals identify their top five strengths. When each team member knows their strengths, discussions can be more focused on how to best contribute to team goals.
- Skills Matrix: Create a visual representation of the skills and expertise available within your team. This can

highlight areas of strength and gaps that might need external support or further development.

- Regular Check-ins: Use one-on-one meetings to discuss and document each team member's perceived strengths and interests. This can also be a platform for team members to express interest in developing new skills.

Strategic Team Assembly

Building a team is like composing a piece of music. It would be best to have the right balance of instruments, playing at the right time, to create harmony. Here's how you can apply this analogy to team assembly:

- Map out the project needs: List down the skills and qualities required for successful project completion.
- Match strengths to roles: Align team members' identified strengths with the project's needs.
- Consider pairing complementary skills: Consider how team members can learn from each other by working together, much like pairing a seasoned expert with a keen learner.

Cultivating a Strengths-Based Culture

Fostering an environment where each member's strengths are recognized and utilized not only enhances team performance but also boosts morale and job satisfaction.

- Strengths-based Development Programs: Implement development programs focused on enhancing individual strengths rather than solely improving weaknesses.

- Recognition: Regularly acknowledge and celebrate when team members use their strengths to contribute to the team's success. This can be done in team meetings, through company-wide communications, or even in informal settings.
- Empowerment: Give team members autonomy to make decisions and take action based on their strengths. This trust can motivate them to take ownership and excel in their roles.

Remember that the magic of a high-performing team lies in its diversity—the unique blend of strengths, talents, and perspectives each member brings. As a leader, your role is to identify, celebrate, and strategically leverage these diverse strengths, creating an environment where everyone can do their best work. By doing so, you not only elevate your team's performance but also contribute to a more inclusive, dynamic, and innovative workplace culture.

5.2 THE ROLE OF TRUST IN TEAM PERFORMANCE

Trust forms the bedrock upon which high-performing teams are built. It's the invisible glue that binds team members together, enabling them to navigate challenges, celebrate successes, and work toward common goals with a shared sense of purpose. Building this foundational element requires deliberate actions and understanding its core components.

Foundations of Trust

At its core, trust within a team is anchored in reliability, understanding, and respect. These elements must be nurtured over time through:

- Reliability: Team members must be able to count on each other to fulfill promises and meet deadlines.
- Understanding: There should be a mutual understanding of each individual's roles, strengths, and how they contribute to the team's objectives.
- Respect: Recognizing and valuing the diverse backgrounds, skills, and perspectives each person brings to the team enhances trust.

For leaders, exemplifying these behaviors sets precedence, encouraging team members to mirror these trustworthy actions in their interactions.

Trust-Building Activities

Creating opportunities for team members to connect more deeply can accelerate the trust-building process. Consider integrating the following activities into your team's routine:

- Team Retreats: Off-site retreats allow team members to interact in a non-work context, fostering personal connections that strengthen professional relationships.
- Trust Circles: Small group discussions where team members share personal stories and experiences can help break down barriers and build empathy.
- Collaborative Challenges: Engage the team in problem-solving exercises or projects that require collaboration. Successfully navigating these challenges together can boost trust through shared accomplishments.

These activities should be designed to encourage openness, vulnerability, and mutual support, laying the groundwork for a trusting team environment.

Maintaining Trust

Maintaining trust is an ongoing effort that hinges on transparency, integrity, and consistent communication. Here are strategies to ensure trust remains strong within your team:

- Regular Updates: Keep the team informed about the project or organization's developments, changes, and challenges. This transparency prevents rumors and misinformation from undermining trust.
- Integrity in Actions: Model integrity by always doing what you say you will do. Leadership acting with honesty and accountability reinforces the importance of these values within the team.
- Open Lines of Communication: Encourage an environment where feedback is freely given and received. Open communication channels ensure misunderstandings are quickly addressed, preventing erosion of trust.

By prioritizing these practices, leaders can cultivate an atmosphere where trust thrives, bolstering team cohesion and performance.

Rebuilding Trust

Trust can be damaged even in the strongest teams due to misunderstandings, broken promises, or failures in accountability. Rebuilding trust requires a commitment to honesty, vulnerability, and corrective action.

- Acknowledge the Issue: The first step in rebuilding trust is acknowledging that a breach has occurred. This requires a willingness to discuss the issue openly and honestly without assigning blame.

- Apologize and Take Responsibility: If the breach of trust stems from your actions, offer a sincere apology and take responsibility. This demonstrates accountability and a commitment to making amends.
- Develop a Plan for Repair: Work together with the affected parties to develop a plan to repair the damage. This might include setting new expectations, creating accountability measures, or implementing changes to prevent future issues.
- Follow Through: The most crucial step in rebuilding trust is to follow through on agreed-upon actions. Consistency in your efforts to repair relationships will show your commitment to restoring trust.

Rebuilding trust takes time and patience. It requires a willingness to confront uncomfortable truths, make necessary changes, and consistently demonstrate through actions that faith can be restored. With a focused effort, teams can overcome breaches in trust, emerging stronger and more unified.

The presence or absence of trust can significantly impact team dynamics and success in high-performing teams. Leaders have a pivotal role in establishing, nurturing, and, when necessary, repairing the trust upon which effective teamwork is built. Through deliberate efforts to foster reliability, understanding, respect, and open communication, leaders can create an environment where trust flourishes, driving team performance to new heights.

5.3 SETTING CLEAR GOALS AND EXPECTATIONS

In the orchestra of team performance, setting the right tempo and key is vital for a harmonious outcome. This is where the importance of establishing clear goals and expectations comes into play. It's about giving each team member a score to follow, ensuring everyone is in tune with the team's overarching mission and objectives.

Goal-Setting Frameworks

Employing proven goal-setting frameworks can ensure the team's efforts are harmonized toward a common objective. One of the most renowned methods is the SMART criteria, which stands for Specific, Measurable, Achievable, Relevant, and Time-bound goals. This framework ensures that objectives are not just wishes but actionable targets the team can realistically achieve within a set timeframe.

- Specific: Goals should be clear and precise, leaving no room for ambiguity about what is expected.
- Measurable: There should be concrete criteria for measuring progress toward achieving each goal.
- Achievable: While goals should be challenging, they must also be attainable to keep the team motivated.
- Relevant: Every goal must matter to the team and align with broader organizational objectives.
- Time-bound: Assigning deadlines ensures that efforts are focused and that there is a sense of urgency in achieving the goals.

Utilizing this framework not only provides a structured approach to goal setting but also facilitates easier communication of these goals to the team, ensuring everyone understands what needs to be accomplished and by when.

Aligning Team With Organizational Goals

For a team to truly excel, its objectives should not exist in a vacuum. Instead, objectives must reflect and contribute to larger organizational goals. Achieving this alignment starts with clearly understanding the company's vision, mission, and strategic objectives.

The next step involves breaking down these broad organizational goals into more specific, departmental, or team-based objectives. This process not only ensures that the team's work contributes directly to the company's success but also helps team members see the value and impact of their contributions. Regular discussions about how team goals fit into the bigger picture reinforce this alignment and keep everyone focused on what truly matters.

Communicating Expectations

Clarity is the key to effective execution. Once goals are set, it is critical to communicate them clearly, concisely, and transparently. This involves more than just outlining goals; it involves explaining why they are important, how they contribute to the larger objectives, and what success looks like.

Here are a few strategies to ensure expectations are communicated effectively:

- Use multiple channels: Recognize that people absorb information in different ways. Utilize a mix of written, verbal, and visual communication tools to share goals and expectations.

- Encourage feedback: After communicating goals and expectations, allow team members to ask questions or express concerns. This can help identify any misunderstandings and provide clarity.
- Reiterate regularly: Goals should be a recurring topic in team meetings, one-on-ones, and other communications. This keeps them at the top of their minds and allows for adjustments as needed.

Monitoring and Adjusting Goals

The path to achieving team goals is rarely linear. Obstacles, changes in the business environment, or shifts in organizational priorities can all impact progress. This makes monitoring and adjusting goals critical for effective goal management.

- Regular check-ins: Schedule periodic reviews of the team's progress toward its goals. Depending on the objectives, these can be weekly, monthly, or quarterly.
- Transparent tracking: Use project management tools or dashboards that allow team members to update their progress. This facilitates easier monitoring and fosters accountability.
- Flexibility: Be willing to adjust goals as needed. If unforeseen circumstances make a particular objective irrelevant or unattainable, it's better to redefine it than to persist with something that no longer serves the team or organization well.

Setting clear goals and expectations is like charting a course for a ship. It requires a captain who can not only map out the destination but also adjust the sails as the wind changes. For leaders, this means not just defining what success looks like but also guiding their teams through the ebbs and flows, ensuring that, regardless of the challenges encountered, the journey remains focused, purposeful, and aligned with the organization's ultimate mission.

5.4 ENCOURAGING INNOVATION AND CREATIVE THINKING

Successful teams are those that can innovate and creatively solve problems. This ability sets them apart in a constantly evolving world. This section explores how leaders can cultivate an atmosphere that welcomes and actively stimulates innovation and creative thinking among their team members.

Fostering an Innovative Environment

Creating a space where innovation thrives involves more than just an open-door policy. It's about building an ecosystem that values curiosity and rewards risk-taking. Here's how:

- Psychological Safety: Ensure that your team feels safe to voice their ideas, no matter how unconventional they may seem. A culture of fear stifles creativity; a culture of psychological safety fertilizes it.
- Autonomy: Give your team the freedom to explore their ideas. Autonomy signals trust and encourages individuals to invest more deeply in their creative pursuits.

Brainstorming and Idea Generation

The brainstorming process is critical in unlocking the creative potential within your team. Here are some techniques to make your brainstorming sessions more productive:

- No Idea is a Bad Idea: Start your sessions with the rule that every idea is welcome, with no judgment. This encourages free thinking and often leads to the most innovative solutions emerging from the most unexpected suggestions.
- The 'Yes, And' Technique: Build on others' ideas with "Yes, and …" rather than shutting them down. This approach fosters collaborative thinking and expands on initial ideas, making them richer and more developed.
- Break Out of the Box: Occasionally, take your brainstorming sessions out of the office environment. Changing physical spaces can stimulate new ways of thinking and inspire creativity.

Implementing Ideas Into Action

The bridge from ideation to implementation is where many creative initiatives falter. To successfully navigate this transition:

- Idea Evaluation: Use criteria that align with your team's goals and values to assess which ideas to pursue. Consider feasibility, impact, and alignment with long-term objectives.
- Prototype and Test: Encourage the development of prototypes or pilot programs. These smaller-scale tests can provide valuable insights and allow for adjustments before full-scale execution.
- Assign Champions: For each idea that moves forward, assign a champion. This person is responsible for guiding the idea from concept to reality, ensuring it has the focus and resources needed.

Celebrating Creative Successes

Recognizing and celebrating your team's innovative achievements is crucial. It rewards those involved and signals to the rest of the team that creative efforts are valued.

- Spotlight Success: Share successful innovations in team meetings or company-wide communications. Detailing the journey from idea to implementation can be incredibly motivating.
- Reward Creativity: Consider establishing a rewards system for innovative ideas that positively impact the team or company. Rewards can range from public recognition to financial bonuses or additional professional development opportunities.
- Encourage Reflection: After a project's completion, encourage the team to reflect on what worked and what didn't. This reflection is a learning opportunity that will prepare the team for even greater success in future projects.

In supporting innovation and creative thinking, the role of a leader is twofold: to create an environment where such qualities can flourish and to guide the process of turning innovative ideas into tangible results. By prioritizing psychological safety, embracing diverse perspectives, and celebrating creative successes, leaders can foster a culture of innovation that drives their team and organization forward.

As we wrap up this exploration, it's evident that the teams poised for success are those that embrace change, seek out fresh perspectives, and dare to think differently. These are the teams that not only adapt to the evolving landscape of their industries but also play pivotal roles in shaping the future. Moving forward, the focus shifts to nurturing team growth and development, where the principles of trust, clear goals, and a culture of innovation continue to underpin a thriving, dynamic team environment.

6

NURTURING TEAM GROWTH AND DEVELOPMENT

Picture a garden in full bloom, with each plant representing a member of your team. Just as gardeners nurture each plant according to its specific needs—pruning, watering, and fertilizing differently—so too must leaders cultivate their team members' growth with personalized care and attention. This thoughtful approach not only fosters individual development but also enriches the entire garden, making the collective more vibrant and productive. This chapter focuses on crafting personalized development plans that catalyze both personal and professional growth, sowing the seeds for a future where each team member achieves their full potential.

6.1 INDIVIDUAL ASSESSMENTS FOR PERSONALIZED PLANS

The foundation of any personalized development plan is understanding each team member's unique aspirations, strengths, and areas for growth. Conducting individual assessments provides this insight. Use a mix of personality tests, skill assessments, and one-on-one conversations to gather information. The key is to approach this process with curiosity and an open mind, aiming to uncover not just where a team member excels or needs improvement but also where their passions lie.

A practical step here is to schedule assessment sessions with each team member. During these sessions, explore their career aspirations, current job satisfaction levels, and perceived personal growth opportunities. Tools like the Myers-Briggs Type Indicator or the StrengthsFinder can supplement these discussions, providing a structured framework to understand each person's inclinations and potential areas for development.

Setting Development Goals

Once you've mapped out an individual's strengths, weaknesses, and aspirations, setting realistic and motivating development goals is the next step. This involves a collaborative process where you and the team member discuss and agree on specific objectives that align with their career aspirations and the team's needs. Effective goals should be challenging yet achievable, with clear milestones and timelines to track progress.

For instance, if a team member aims to improve their public speaking skills, a development goal could be to lead a presentation in a team meeting within the next three months. This goal is specific, time-bound, and directly tied to the team member's broader aspiration to enhance their communication abilities.

Resources for Development

Identifying the right resources is crucial for turning development goals into reality. These resources might include online courses, workshops, books, mentoring, or job-shadowing opportunities. It's about matching the right tool to the goal.

Suppose a team member wants to learn a new software relevant to their role. You could provide access to an online course, allocate time during their workweek for learning, and pair them with a mentor who is proficient in the software. This approach not only supports their education but also demonstrates the organization's investment in their growth.

A helpful tactic is creating a resource list that team members can access. This list could categorize resources based on different development areas, such as leadership skills, technical proficiency, or creative thinking. Regularly update this list with new findings and encourage team members to contribute resources they've found beneficial.

Tracking and Evaluating Progress

Monitoring progress toward development goals is essential for maintaining momentum and making adjustments as needed. This could take the form of regular check-ins where you discuss progress, challenges, and next steps. These check-ins provide an opportunity to celebrate achievements, no matter how small, and to recalibrate goals if circumstances have changed.

Consider using a simple tracking tool or spreadsheet. In this tool, you and the team member can update progress on goals and note any resources used or milestones achieved. This visual representation of progress can be incredibly motivating and also helps evaluate the effectiveness of the development plan over time.

In fostering team growth and development, remember that the goal is not just to fill gaps or improve performance. It's about empowering each team member to explore their potential fully, contributing to their fulfillment and the team's success. Like the gardener who tends to each plant's needs, your role as a leader is to provide the right conditions for each team member to flourish, creating a thriving, dynamic team garden.

6.2 THE POWER OF CONSTRUCTIVE FEEDBACK

In team dynamics, feedback is like a thread running through and intertwining with growth, learning, and development. Establishing a culture that not only accepts but actively seeks constructive feedback can transform potential into excellence. This section explores the strategies and practices that underpin the effective exchange of feedback, laying the groundwork for a team culture characterized by continuous improvement and open communication.

Creating a Feedback Culture

At the heart of a thriving team lies a culture where feedback is viewed not as criticism but as a gift—a tool for growth and improvement. Cultivating this culture starts with leadership. When leaders openly request feedback on their decisions and actions, they signal that feedback is not just welcomed but valued. This openness sets the stage for a team environment where feedback flows freely without fear of retribution or negative consequences.

To weave feedback into the fabric of your team's culture, consider these practices:

- Model the behavior you seek: Regularly ask for feedback on your leadership and projects, demonstrating how to receive and act on it positively.

- Normalize feedback: Integrate feedback into daily routines and interactions, making it a natural part of how your team communicates and works together.
- Educate on the value of feedback: Share stories and examples of how feedback has led to positive changes and improvements, both within and outside your organization.

Techniques for Giving and Receiving Feedback

Navigating the art of feedback requires finesse—knowing how to deliver feedback that inspires growth and how to accept input with openness. Here are some techniques to guide both processes:

For Giving Feedback:

- Be specific and objective: Focus on behaviors and outcomes rather than personal attributes. Specify what was done and its impact, and suggest actionable steps for improvement or growth.
- Use a positive frame: Frame feedback in a way that highlights opportunities for growth and improvement. Start by acknowledging what went well before addressing areas for development.
- Timing and setting matter: Choose an appropriate time and a private setting for feedback discussions to ensure the receiver is receptive and not put on the spot.

For Receiving Feedback:

- Listen actively: Approach feedback with an open mind, seeking to understand the shared perspective without rushing to defend or explain.

- Ask clarifying questions: If feedback isn't clear, ask questions that help you understand the specifics and the desired outcomes.
- Express appreciation: Thank the person for their feedback, acknowledging the time and thought they've put into sharing their observations with you.

Feedback as a Development Tool

When leveraged effectively, feedback transcends its role as a communication tool, becoming a catalyst for personal and professional development. It illuminates blind spots, reinforces strengths, and provides a roadmap for growth. To harness feedback as a development tool:

- Link feedback to development goals: Connect the dots between the feedback received and the individual's development goals, illustrating how addressing the feedback can help achieve these goals.
- Create action plans based on feedback: Work together with team members to develop action plans that address feedback, specifying steps, resources, and timelines for improvement.
- Reflect and adjust: Encourage team members to regularly reflect on the feedback and their progress, adjusting their action plans as needed based on new insights and results.

Regular Feedback Sessions

Instituting regular, structured feedback sessions ensures that feedback isn't left to chance encounters but is an integral part of your team's rhythm. These sessions—whether weekly one-on-ones, monthly group reviews, or quarterly performance discussions—

provide a consistent framework for open dialogue, fostering an environment of ongoing improvement and learning.

To maximize the effectiveness of these sessions:

- Prepare: Encourage both parties to prepare for feedback sessions by reflecting on achievements, challenges, and areas for growth since the last discussion.
- Structure: Use a structured format for these sessions that covers accomplishments, challenges faced, feedback on recent projects, and development progress.
- Follow-up: Conclude each session with clear next steps and follow up on these in subsequent meetings to ensure continuity and accountability.

In cultivating a team environment where constructive feedback is a valued mechanism for growth, leaders lay the foundation for continuous improvement, innovation, and development. This culture of feedback not only propels individuals toward their full potential but also drives the team toward collective success and excellence.

6.3 FACILITATING TEAM LEARNING OPPORTUNITIES

In the evolving landscape of team development, cultivating a learning culture is a pivotal element for promoting both individual growth and collective success. This segment explores the multifaceted approach to nurturing learning within a team, focusing on recognizing learning needs, leveraging diverse educational formats and platforms, encouraging autonomous learning endeavors, and enhancing knowledge sharing among team members.

Identifying Learning Needs

The first step in cultivating a fertile learning environment is accurately identifying your team's learning needs. This process goes beyond surface-level assessments, delving into both the team's collective aspirations and its members' individual ambitions. Begin with an open dialogue, inviting team members to express areas where they feel confident, as well as those where they seek improvement. Supplement these discussions with performance data and project outcomes to pinpoint skills gaps and opportunities for growth. Tools such as skill heat maps can visually represent where your team's strengths lie and where fertile ground for development exists.

Learning Formats and Platforms

Once you clearly understand your team's learning needs, the next step is to match these requirements with appropriate learning formats and platforms. The digital age offers a plethora of educational resources, from online courses on platforms like Coursera and Udemy to interactive workshops and webinars provided by industry leaders. Consider the following when choosing the right format:

- Workshops and Seminars: Ideal for interactive learning and skill development in a collaborative setting. Look for opportunities that offer hands-on experience and real-world application.
- Online Courses and Webinars: These provide flexibility, allowing team members to learn at their own pace and on their own schedule. Many platforms also offer courses created by universities and leading companies, ensuring high-quality content.

- Cross-Training: Organize sessions where team members can learn from each other. This not only supports skill development but also fosters team cohesion and understanding of different roles within the project.

Encouraging Self-Directed Learning

Empowering team members to take charge of their learning journey is critical to fostering a culture of growth. Encourage team members to set personal learning goals and explore topics that pique their interest, even if they fall outside their immediate job responsibilities. Here are a few strategies to promote self-directed learning:

- Learning Budgets: Allocate a budget for individual learning and development. This can be used for courses, books, or attending conferences, providing team members with the resources they need to pursue their learning goals.
- Personal Learning Projects: Allow team members to work on projects or research topics of personal interest during the workweek. This not only motivates learning but can also lead to innovative ideas and solutions for the team.

Sharing Knowledge Among Team Members

The final piece of the puzzle in building a learning-centric team environment is facilitating the exchange of knowledge among team members. This not only amplifies the impact of individual learning efforts but also enriches the team's collective knowledge base. Implement practices such as:

- Peer-to-Peer Training: Schedule regular sessions where team members can teach each other new skills or share insights from recent learning experiences. This could be in the form of short presentations, workshops, or informal discussions.
- Lunch and Learn Sessions: Organize informal learning sessions over lunch where team members can discuss interesting topics and recent learnings or even invite external speakers. This relaxed setting encourages participation and makes learning a part of the team's routine.
- Knowledge Repository: Create a shared digital space where team members can contribute learning materials, articles, course recommendations, and project learnings. This ensures valuable knowledge is accessible to everyone and can be built upon over time.

In fostering a team culture that values and promotes learning, you pave the way for continuous improvement, innovation, and resilience. It's about creating an environment where curiosity is encouraged, knowledge is shared freely, and every team member is empowered to explore their potential. Through a thoughtful blend of identifying learning needs, utilizing diverse learning formats, encouraging self-directed learning pursuits, and enhancing knowledge sharing, you set the stage for a team that not only grows together but also thrives together.

6.4 RECOGNIZING AND CELEBRATING TEAM ACHIEVEMENTS

In a world where the pace of work often demands relentless forward motion, pausing to acknowledge the milestones and successes achieved along the way is a vital practice. Recognition serves as the fuel that powers the engine of motivation, propelling teams toward sustained high performance. This section illuminates the pivotal role of celebrating both individual efforts and collective triumphs, offering insights into the diverse strategies for recognition and the impact of consistent acknowledgment of team dynamics.

The Value of Acknowledgment

At its heart, recognizing achievements is about seeing and affirming the value of the work and the person behind it. Whether it's a personal milestone such as mastering a new skill or a team achievement, acknowledgment reinforces the significance of these accomplishments. This validation can greatly enhance morale, fostering a culture where effort and success are noticed and appreciated. More so, it serves as a powerful motivator, encouraging ongoing commitment and effort toward future objectives.

Strategies for Effective Recognition

Recognition can take many forms, each resonating differently with individuals and teams. Here are some practical ways to incorporate recognition into your leadership approach:

- Personalized Praise: Tailor your recognition to the individual. Some may appreciate public acknowledgment during team meetings, while others might prefer a personal note or one-on-one commendation.
- Formal Awards: Establish awards for various achievement categories, such as 'Innovator of the Month' or 'Team Player Award.' These formal recognitions can become highly anticipated events that highlight exceptional contributions.

- Peer Recognition Programs: Implement a system that allows team members to recognize each other's efforts and accomplishments. Peer recognition can be incredibly meaningful, fostering a supportive team environment.
- Digital Kudos: Utilize digital platforms or team communication tools to share kudos or shout-outs. This method allows for real-time recognition and can be seen by the entire team, enhancing the sense of community.

Rituals of Celebration

Marking milestones and significant achievements with celebration not only honors the accomplishment but also strengthens team unity and camaraderie. Consider these ideas for commemorating team successes:

- Achievement Ceremonies: Host regular events or ceremonies to celebrate milestones and achievements. These could range from informal team lunches to more formal award ceremonies.
- Milestone Markers: For long-term projects, celebrate reaching significant markers or phases. This could involve a small celebration or a symbolic gesture, such as ringing a bell or placing a pin on a progress board.
- Victory Laps: Encourage team members to share their successes, both big and small, in team meetings. This practice, often referred to as a 'victory lap,' allows the team to collectively acknowledge and celebrate each win.

Leaders can illuminate the path toward continued growth, unity, and excellence by weaving the threads of recognition and celebration into the fabric of team culture. Acknowledging achievements, both big and small, not only validates the effort and passion invested by team members but also cements a collective identity rooted in success and shared purpose. As we move forward, the focus shifts to navigating organizational change—a journey where the principles of trust, clear goals, a culture of innovation, and the power of recognition play integral roles in guiding teams through transitions with resilience and adaptability.

MAKE A DIFFERENCE WITH YOUR REVIEW

UNLOCK THE POWER OF GENEROSITY

"You can give without loving, but you cannot love without giving."

— AMY CARMICHAEL

Imagine stepping into a new role, the excitement mingled with the nerve-wracking realization of responsibility—this is the precipice many leaders find themselves on, unsure and needing guidance. That's where "Effective Leadership Skills for Managers" by J.A. Lough comes in, designed to not just guide but empower new and seasoned leaders alike.

We believe in helping each other, and your generosity could be the guiding light for someone on the brink of their leadership journey. Would you extend a helping hand by sharing your thoughts about this book?

Think of someone like you, perhaps less experienced, who is eager to make a difference but doesn't know where to start. Your review could be the beacon they need.

Our mission is clear: to make "Effective Leadership Skills for Managers" accessible to all. We aim to reach every aspiring leader, and we can only achieve this with your help.

Most people do judge a book by its cover—and its reviews. So, on behalf of a future leader you might never meet, I'm asking you to help by leaving a review. This simple act of kindness—taking less than 60 seconds—can profoundly impact another's career and life. Your words could help:

- One more small business thrive.
- One more entrepreneur achieve their dreams.
- One more employee find purpose in their work.
- One more client overcome their challenges.
- One more vision become a reality.

To contribute your review, simply scan the QR code below and share your experience:

If the thought of assisting a fellow leader excites you, then you are indeed one of us. Welcome aboard! I look forward to helping you explore and master the effective leadership strategies detailed in this book.

Thank you from the depth of my heart. Let's continue this journey together.

- Your biggest fan, J.A. Lough

PS - Remember, when you offer value to someone, your own value increases in their eyes. If you think this book could help another leader, why not send a copy their way? It's another beautiful way to spread goodwill and leadership.

7

NAVIGATING THE WINDS OF CHANGE

Imagine you're at the helm of a ship, navigating through foggy seas. The fog represents the uncertainties that change brings into our professional lives. Just as a seasoned captain uses a compass, maps, and the stars to guide their ship to harbor safely, effective communication is our navigational tool through the fog of organizational change.

7.1 COMMUNICATING CHANGE EFFECTIVELY

Strategic Planning

Strategic planning is the key to successfully steering your team through the waters of change. Clear, well-thought-out plans act as your compass, ensuring every team member understands the direction and the steps needed to get there. When planning how to communicate change, consider the following:

- Map Out the Change Process: Break down the change into stages. Identify key messages, the best communication channels, and the timing for each stage.
- Anticipate Questions and Concerns: Put yourself in your team's shoes. What questions would you have? Addressing these proactively can alleviate concerns and prevent misinformation.

Transparency

Transparency isn't just about being open; it's about being clear about why changes are happening, how they will unfold, and the expected outcomes. Transparency builds trust and helps team members understand the reasons behind decisions, even if they don't fully agree with them. For instance, if a new software is being introduced, don't just announce its arrival. Explain why it was chosen, how it will benefit the team, and offer a clear timeline for its implementation.

Regular Updates

Just as a captain regularly updates their crew on the ship's progress and any course changes, leaders must provide regular updates on the change process. This keeps everyone informed, engaged, and aligned. Consider the following for effective updates:

- Consistent Schedule: Whether weekly, bi-weekly, or monthly, stick to a regular schedule for updates to ensure team members know when to expect new information.
- Multiple Formats: Some team members may prefer emails, while others might find quick video updates more engaging. Use a variety of formats to reach everyone.

- Progress Tracking: Share how the change is progressing. This could be through a simple progress bar in emails, a section in team meetings, or a dashboard on the team's intranet.

Navigating through change is undeniably challenging, yet with the right communication strategies, you can guide your team through it successfully. By planning strategically, ensuring transparency, establishing feedback channels, and providing regular updates, you create a roadmap that not only directs but also supports your team throughout the journey of change.

7.2 MANAGING TEAM EMOTIONS DURING CHANGE

Amid change, a team's emotional landscape can become as varied and unpredictable as the weather. Even positive changes can stir up a mix of responses, from anxiety and resistance to excitement and anticipation. Recognizing and addressing these emotional responses with empathy and support is crucial for maintaining a healthy team dynamic during transitions.

Emotional Intelligence

Leveraging emotional intelligence during periods of change means tuning into your team's subtle cues about their emotional state. This involves more than just observing outward reactions; it requires understanding the underlying feelings those reactions might be masking. For instance, resistance to a new process might stem from fear of inadequacy rather than opposition to the change itself.

- Active Listening: Engage in active listening sessions where team members can express their thoughts and emotions about the change. Listening without immediate judgment or solutions can validate their feelings and provide insights into their concerns.

- Empathy in Action: Show empathy by acknowledging the challenges of the change and sharing your own feelings about the transition, making it clear that it's okay to feel uncertain or apprehensive.

Support Systems

Creating a support structure provides a safety net for team members, offering them resources and strategies to manage the stress or anxiety that change can bring.

- Peer Support Groups: Establish peer support groups within the team. These groups can offer a space for sharing coping strategies and mutual encouragement, reinforcing the idea that no one is alone in their experience of change.
- Professional Resources: Provide access to professional counseling services or stress management workshops. Making these resources available can help team members develop healthy coping mechanisms.
- Flexible Schedules: Allow for flexible work schedules if possible. This flexibility can help team members feel more in control and less overwhelmed during periods of transition.

Positive Reinforcement

Highlighting the benefits of change and reinforcing how it aligns with the team's values and goals can shift perspectives from apprehension to anticipation. Positive reinforcement involves recognizing and celebrating team members' efforts to adapt to change.

- Highlight Success Stories: Share stories of individuals or teams that have successfully navigated similar changes. These stories can inspire and provide practical strategies for adaptation.
- Link Changes to Personal Growth: Make the connection between the change and its potential for personal development clear. For example, a new project management tool might offer team members the chance to enhance their technical skills or lead more significant parts of a project.
- Recognize Efforts: Acknowledge and reward efforts to embrace change, no matter how small. This could range from verbal acknowledgment in team meetings to small tokens of appreciation or incentive rewards.

In navigating the emotional currents of change, the goal is to create an environment where feelings are acknowledged, support is readily available, and the positive aspects of change are brought to the forefront. Through emotional intelligence, supportive structures, open dialogue, and positive reinforcement, leaders can guide their teams through the uncertainties of change with empathy and understanding, fostering resilience and adaptability.

7.3 LEADING BY EXAMPLE: MODELING ADAPTABILITY

In the ever-evolving landscape of organizational change, the beacon guiding a team's course often shines from the actions and attitudes of its leader. Modeling adaptability isn't merely about embracing change personally; it's about embodying the resilience, openness, and agility that inspires your team to navigate transitions confidently and positively.

Personal Adaptability

A leader's ability to adapt to changing circumstances sets the tone for the entire team. When you approach new challenges with enthusiasm rather than apprehension, you signal to your team that change is not just inevitable but a valuable opportunity for growth. Consider the scenario of shifting to a new project management tool. Rather than focusing on the learning curve, highlight the tool's potential to streamline workflows and foster collaboration. Your optimistic outlook can turn apprehension into anticipation.

- Reflect on Past Changes: Share stories of past changes you've navigated, focusing on the challenges you faced and how you overcame them. This not only humanizes you but also demonstrates that obstacles can be surmounted with a positive mindset.
- Show Willingness to Learn: Let your team see you learning the new systems or processes firsthand. Your commitment to understanding and mastering new skills underscores the importance of adaptability.

Visible Leadership

Visibility in leadership becomes even more critical during times of change. Staying engaged with your team, being present in meetings, and actively participating in the change process reassures your team that they are not alone. Your presence is a steady hand on the tiller, guiding and steadying the ship.

- Regular Check-ins: Schedule frequent check-ins with your team to discuss their concerns, progress, and insights about the change. These conversations can provide valuable feedback and demonstrate your commitment to supporting them through the transition.

- Lead by Doing: Take on tasks directly affected by the change, working alongside your team. This not only provides you with firsthand experience of the changes but also shows your team that you are fully invested in the process.

Learning Mindset

Adopting a learning mindset in the face of change is like turning the map around, seeing not just the obstacles but the new paths and possibilities. Emphasize the importance of learning from each stage of the change process, both successes and setbacks. This approach encourages your team to view change as a series of learning opportunities, fostering a culture of continuous improvement.

- Share Learning Moments: Share what you've learned with your team after tackling a new challenge or reaching a milestone in the change process. Discuss both what worked and what didn't, emphasizing the value of each experience in fostering growth.
- Encourage Curiosity: Promote an environment where questions are encouraged and curiosity is valued. When team members feel comfortable asking questions and exploring new ideas, it fuels innovation and adaptability.

Consistency in Leadership

In the swirling currents of change, consistency in leadership provides a much-needed anchor. Maintaining consistency in your values, expectations, and communication reassures your team that some things remain steadfast. This stability is crucial for building trust and confidence during uncertain times.

- Stay True to Core Values: Ensure that your actions and decisions during the change process align with the team's and organization's core values. This alignment reinforces a sense of continuity and purpose.
- Maintain Open Communication: Keep the lines of communication open and consistent. Even when there's no new information to report, regular updates keep everyone on the same page and prevent rumors or uncertainty from undermining the team's morale.

By leading by example through adaptability, you illuminate the path forward for your team during times of change. Your personal adaptability inspires resilience, your visible leadership offers guidance and reassurance, embracing a learning mindset fosters a culture of growth and innovation, and your consistency in leadership ensures a foundation of trust and stability. By embodying these principles, you not only navigate the currents of change successfully but also empower your team to do the same, turning transition challenges into opportunities for development and achievement.

7.4 KEEPING THE TEAM FOCUSED AND MOTIVATED

In an environment of change, maintaining team focus and motivation can often feel like trying to navigate a ship through a stormy sea. The key to smooth sailing lies not just in the strength of the ship but in the unity and morale of its crew. Here's how leaders can ensure their teams remain undeterred and driven, even when the waters get rough.

Clear Goals and Objectives

First and foremost, clarity in goals and objectives serves as the North Star for teams navigating change. The path forward becomes much easier to chart when the destination is clear. Here's how to ensure these goals are as effective as beacons in the night:

- Define with Precision: Goals should be as sharp as a lighthouse beam, cutting through the fog of uncertainty and illuminating the way forward. Ensure they are specific enough that every team member can articulate not just the what but the why behind their daily tasks.
- Make Them Measurable: Attach metrics and milestones to these goals. This not only helps in tracking progress but also provides tangible markers of success for the team to celebrate.
- Align with Larger Vision: Ensure these objectives are not isolated buoys but are linked to the organization's broader vision. This alignment helps team members see the value and impact of their contributions beyond the immediate horizon.

Personal Development Opportunities

Finally, change offers fertile ground for growth, not just for the organization but for individuals as well. Highlighting and providing opportunities for personal development can turn a potentially unsettling time into an exciting one. Here's how:

- Spotlight Growth: Make clear how the change will provide opportunities for each team member to grow. Highlight these prospects, such as learning new skills, taking on more responsibility, or exploring new business areas.

- Provide Resources: Offer access to training, workshops, or courses to help team members develop the skills needed to thrive in the new environment. This not only aids in personal growth but also benefits the organization.
- Encourage Exploration: Support team members interested in exploring new roles or projects as part of the change. This flexibility can uncover hidden talents and drive innovation within the team.

By implementing these strategies, leaders can ensure their teams remain focused and motivated through the winds of change. This approach not only helps navigate the present storm but also prepares the team for future voyages, equipped with stronger bonds, sharpened skills, and an unbreakable spirit.

As we draw the curtains on this chapter, let's remember that change, while challenging, is also a gateway to new beginnings and opportunities. It's a chance to redefine, grow, and emerge stronger. With a clear map, a motivated and cohesive crew, and a ship full of individuals ready to grow, the journey ahead is one filled with promise. As we set our sights on the next chapter, we carry forward the lessons of resilience, adaptability, and the enduring power of a team united in purpose and spirit.

8

OVERCOMING LEADERSHIP CHALLENGES

Imagine a theater production in full swing, actors on stage, and the director behind the scenes ensuring every cue is met with precision. Now, picture a scene where the script suddenly changes, an actor misses a cue, or a prop isn't where it should be. It's in these moments that the director's role becomes crucial—not just directing the play but navigating through unexpected challenges, ensuring the show goes on seamlessly. Similarly, leadership involves not just directing a team toward predefined goals but also managing the unforeseen hiccups and conflicts that inevitably arise. How a leader handles these moments can either strengthen the team or lead to discord.

8.1. RESOLVING CONFLICTS WITHIN THE TEAM

Conflict Resolution Strategies

No two conflicts are the same, and as such, having a toolkit of conflict resolution strategies is vital. Key strategies include:

- Active Listening: Ensure all parties feel heard. This involves summarizing what you've heard to confirm understanding, demonstrating empathy, and avoiding premature judgment.
- Identifying Underlying Needs: Often, conflicts stem from unmet needs. Identifying these can shift the focus from winning arguments to finding solutions.
- Solution-Focused Approach: Encourage a shift from dwelling on the problem to collaboratively brainstorming solutions.

Mediation and Facilitation

Sometimes, a neutral party can help facilitate resolution. As a leader, acting as a mediator involves:

- Setting clear rules for the mediation process, ensuring respect and confidentiality.
- Helping parties articulate their perspectives without interruption.
- Guiding the conversation toward understanding and compromise.

Building a Collaborative Environment

A proactive approach to conflict involves cultivating an environment where team members feel comfortable expressing dissenting opinions. This includes:

- Regular team-building activities that emphasize collaboration and trust.
- Encourage open communication and model it by sharing your thoughts and concerns openly.

- Setting clear expectations about respectful disagreement and constructive criticism.

Learning from Conflict

Every conflict presents a learning opportunity. Reflecting on conflicts can provide insights into team dynamics, personal leadership style, and areas for improvement. Consider:

- Holding a debrief session with your team after resolving a conflict to discuss lessons learned.
- Encouraging team members to share their takeaways and how the experience will influence future interactions.
- Reflecting personally on your role in the conflict and resolution process. What worked well? What could have been handled differently?

Visual Element: Conflict Resolution Flowchart

A flowchart can visually guide leaders through the steps of resolving team conflicts, from identifying the issue to implementing and reviewing solutions. A flowchart serves as a quick reference in the heat of the moment, ensuring key steps aren't overlooked.

Interactive Element: Conflict Scenarios Role-Play

Role-playing exercises based on hypothetical conflict scenarios can provide valuable practice in handling difficult conversations and mediating disputes. This could be facilitated in leadership workshops or team meetings, allowing for feedback and discussion of different approaches.

Textual Element: Checklist for Constructive Conflict Resolution

Ensure all parties have the opportunity to share their perspective without interruption.

- Identify the underlying needs or concerns driving the conflict.
- Focus on interests, not positions.
- Brainstorm possible solutions that address the needs of all parties involved.
- Agree on a solution and outline the steps to implement it.
- Set a follow-up meeting to assess the effectiveness of the solution.

While challenging, conflict is an inevitable part of team dynamics. It's not the presence of conflict but how it's handled that defines a team's resilience and cohesion. Leaders can navigate these challenges by employing effective resolution strategies, facilitating open communication, and viewing conflicts as opportunities for growth, fostering a stronger, more unified team. Remember, the goal isn't to avoid conflict but to manage it in a way that enriches the team's experience and bonds.

8.2. DEALING WITH UNDERPERFORMANCE CONSTRUCTIVELY

When a ship faces turbulent waters, it's not just the strength of the winds or the height of the waves that matters but also how well each crew member performs their role. In leadership, encountering underperformance within a team is much like navigating these choppy seas. The approach taken to lift performance levels can significantly influence the journey's success and the team's morale. Let's explore the steps to address underperformance with a focus on support and growth.

Identifying Root Causes

Before charting a course for improvement, understanding why a team member may be underperforming is crucial. This requires looking beyond surface-level symptoms to uncover underlying issues, ranging from personal challenges outside of work to mismatches in role expectations. Conducting a thorough analysis involves:

- Engaging in open, empathetic conversations to explore any external factors affecting performance.
- Reviewing role expectations and alignment with the individual's skills and interests.
- Assessing the team dynamics and work environment to identify possible influences on performance.
- This exploration should be approached with sensitivity and confidentiality, ensuring the team member feels supported throughout the process.

Personalized Improvement Plans

Once the underlying causes of underperformance are understood, creating a tailored improvement plan can provide a clear path forward. This plan should be collaborative, involving both the leader and the team member in setting achievable goals. Essential components of an effective plan include:

- Specific, measurable objectives that provide clarity on what success looks like.

- A realistic timeline that allows for meaningful progress without overwhelming the individual.
- Identified resources or support mechanisms, such as training opportunities, mentorship, or role adjustments.

The key is to frame this plan not as a punitive measure but as a roadmap to success, emphasizing the belief in the individual's ability to grow and improve.

Regular Check-Ins and Support

Continuous support is vital for maintaining momentum and making adjustments as needed. Regular check-ins provide an opportunity to celebrate progress, address challenges, and refine the improvement plan based on real-time feedback. These sessions can:

- Foster an ongoing dialogue about the individual's experiences and feelings regarding their progress.
- Offer immediate recognition for improvements, no matter how small, reinforcing positive behaviors and outcomes.
- Allow for swift course corrections if certain strategies are not yielding the expected results.

The frequency and format of these check-ins should be tailored to the individual's preferences and the specifics of the improvement plan, ensuring they are constructive and encouraging.

Fostering a Growth Mindset

Central to the process of addressing underperformance is the cultivation of a growth mindset—the belief that abilities and intelligence can be developed through dedication and hard work. Leaders can foster this mindset by:

- Highlighting examples of personal growth and learning within the team, demonstrating that challenges can be overcome.
- Encouraging an environment where mistakes are seen as learning opportunities rather than failures.
- Providing consistent, positive feedback that focuses on effort and improvement rather than just outcomes.

This approach not only improves performance but also builds resilience and a culture of continuous learning within the team.

The goal in navigating the delicate waters of underperformance is to uplift and support, transforming potential obstacles into opportunities for development. Through understanding, tailored improvement plans, ongoing support, and a focus on growth, leaders can turn the tide on underperformance, guiding their team members back to a course of success and fulfillment.

8.3. BALANCING LEADERSHIP AND PERSONAL LIFE

Navigating the demands of leadership while keeping a harmonious personal life can feel like walking a tightrope. With the wind of responsibilities gusting from both sides, maintaining balance is both an art and a necessity. Here, we will explore the framework not just to walk but to stride confidently across this rope, ensuring a fulfilling professional journey alongside a rich personal life.

Setting Boundaries

The foundation of this balance lies in clear boundaries. These invisible lines enable leaders to compartmentalize, ensuring work stresses don't seep into home life and vice versa. Implementing these boundaries requires:

- Defined Work Hours: Stick to a schedule that clearly demarcates work from personal time. Inform your team and set an example by not sending emails or making work calls outside these hours unless absolutely necessary.
- Physical Separation: If possible, designate a workspace that's separate from personal spaces. This physical distinction helps people mentally switch off from work.
- Communication Guidelines: Establish clear expectations about communication after hours with your team. Emergencies happen, but not everything qualifies as one.

Crafting these boundaries not just for yourself but also respecting them for your team cultivates a culture of mutual respect for personal time, reducing burnout and fostering a healthier work-life balance.

Time Management Techniques

Efficiently managing time allows leaders to fulfill their roles without compromising on personal commitments and well-being. Some effective techniques include:

- Prioritization: Utilize tools like the Eisenhower Box to categorize tasks by urgency and importance. This helps focus on what truly matters, reducing time wasted on less critical activities.

- Batching Tasks: Group similar tasks together and tackle them in dedicated time blocks. This approach minimizes context switching, a notorious time-waster.
- Technology Leverage: Embrace technology for better time management. Apps for task management, scheduling, and reminders can automate routine tasks, freeing up time for strategic thinking and personal pursuits.

When consistently applied, these strategies transform time from a scarce commodity to a resource effectively utilized for professional success and personal fulfillment.

Self-Care Practices

Self-care is the fuel that powers the engine of leadership. Neglecting this aspect can lead to burnout, affecting decision-making, creativity, and overall performance. Regular self-care practices that support physical, mental, and emotional well-being include:

- Physical Activity: Incorporate regular exercise into your routine. Whether it's a morning jog, yoga, or a workout session, physical activity is a proven stress reliever.
- Mindfulness and Meditation: Daily mindfulness or meditation practices can significantly reduce stress levels, enhance focus, and improve emotional regulation.
- Hobbies and Interests: Engage in activities outside of work that bring joy and relaxation. Whether reading, painting, or gardening, hobbies offer a healthy escape and a means to recharge.

Adopting these self-care practices ensures that leaders remain effective not only in their roles but also as happy and healthy individuals outside of work.

Delegation and Trust

Delegation is not a sign of weakness but a hallmark of strong leadership. It involves trusting your team with responsibilities, empowering them to make decisions, and freeing up your time for high-level strategic work and personal rejuvenation. Effective delegation includes:

- Identifying Strengths and Weaknesses: Match tasks with team members' strengths. This not only ensures tasks are completed efficiently but also contributes to team members' growth and job satisfaction.
- Clear Expectations: When delegating, be clear about the outcomes you expect, the timeline, and the extent of decision-making authority.
- Feedback and Support: Provide constructive feedback and be available for support, but resist the urge to micromanage. Trust your team to deliver, giving them room to navigate challenges and learn in the process.

Building a trustworthy team and mastering the art of delegation not only enhances team performance but also creates the space leaders need to enjoy a rich personal life, ensuring they remain inspired, motivated, and balanced.

Navigating leadership with an eye toward a fulfilling personal life is not for the faint-hearted. It demands deliberate action in setting boundaries, managing time efficiently, committing to self-care, and fostering a team you can trust and delegate to. This approach ensures sustained professional success and guarantees a rewarding and enriching personal life, allowing leaders to thrive in all facets of life.

8.4. LEADING REMOTE TEAMS SUCCESSFULLY

In the fabric of modern leadership, the thread of managing remote teams weaves a complex pattern, challenging yet rich with opportunity. The digital age has ushered in a paradigm shift, where the physical office space is no longer the epicenter of our work universe. This new reality brings to the forefront the need for adeptness in virtual communication, trust-building from afar, nurturing team spirit without shared physical spaces, and ensuring productivity without infringing on personal autonomy.

Effective Virtual Communication

The lifeline of remote teams is virtual communication. Without the nuances of face-to-face interaction, every chat message, email, or video call must be optimized to convey clear, concise, and considerate messages. Tools and platforms that facilitate seamless communication become invaluable assets. However, it's not just about having the right tools; it's also about using them smartly:

- Schedule regular video meetings to maintain a visual connection, which can help you pick up nonverbal cues often lost in written communication.
- Encourage an 'audio-video-on' culture during meetings to foster a sense of presence and engagement.
- Adopt a platform that integrates various forms of communication (chat, video, document sharing) to reduce toggling between applications.

- Establish communication guidelines, such as response time expectations, appropriate message hours, and the preferred platform for different types of communication.

Building Trust Remotely

Trust becomes even more pivotal when teams are dispersed. It's the invisible cord that ties the team together, ensuring that despite the physical distance, everyone is working toward common goals with shared enthusiasm. Building this trust remotely hinges on clarity and reliability:

- Clearly define roles, responsibilities, and expectations from the get-go. Ambiguity can be the quicksand of remote work, pulling down productivity and morale.
- Utilize project management tools that allow for transparent tracking of tasks and progress. This visibility can help build accountability and reassure team members that their contributions are recognized.
- Make a point of publicly acknowledging and celebrating achievements and milestones within the team. This not only builds trust but also fosters a culture of appreciation and accountability.
- Be consistent in your actions and follow through. Reliability from leadership reinforces trust and sets the standard for the team.

Fostering Team Spirit Virtually

Creating a sense of belonging and camaraderie in a virtual environment requires creativity and effort. Without the watercooler chats or spontaneous lunch outings, leaders must intentionally craft opportunities for informal interaction and connection:

- Host virtual coffee breaks or happy hours where the conversation is not about work. This can help team members connect on a personal level.
- Celebrate birthdays, work anniversaries, and personal milestones in team calls or through digital cards signed by everyone.
- Initiate virtual team-building activities that are not just fun but also underscore collaboration and problem-solving. Think along the lines of online escape rooms or trivia contests.
- Encourage peer recognition programs where team members can highlight each other's contributions and successes.

Monitoring and Supporting Remote Work

While overseeing a remote team, striking the right balance between ensuring productivity and respecting personal autonomy is key. Leaders need to foster an environment where team members feel supported in their tasks and trusted to manage their time effectively:

- Implement regular one-on-one check-ins focusing on support and development, not just task progress. Use this time to discuss challenges, offer help, and understand the individual's work environment.
- Respect boundaries by not expecting immediate responses to messages sent outside of agreed-upon working hours unless previously discussed for urgent matters.
- Encourage team members to share their work setups and offer suggestions for improvements, whether software tools or ergonomic chairs.

- Promote flexibility in working hours, recognizing that remote work can offer the advantage of working during hours when individuals feel most productive.

As we wrap up this exploration into leading remote teams, we touch upon the essence of modern leadership—adaptability, empathy, and a keen sense of how to harness technology not just for productivity but as a bridge to connect, inspire, and support. These principles don't just apply to remote teams but are reflective of a broader shift in the world of work, one that values results and well-being in equal measure. Looking ahead, the leadership landscape continues to evolve, presenting new challenges and opportunities to redefine what it means to lead and succeed in an increasingly connected world.

9

BUILDING YOUR LEADERSHIP IDENTITY

Picture a mosaic, each piece distinct, coming together to form a complete, vivid image. This mosaic represents your leadership identity, composed of your values, experiences, and philosophies. Unlike a painting that is complete upon the last stroke, this mosaic continually evolves as you add new pieces throughout your career. It's this dynamic, ever-changing nature of leadership that makes it both a challenge and a privilege to pursue. In this chapter, we dive into the foundational layer of this mosaic: defining your leadership philosophy.

9.1. DEFINING YOUR LEADERSHIP PHILOSOPHY

Personal Values as a Foundation

Your leadership philosophy is deeply rooted in your personal values. These values act as the compass that guides your decisions, actions, and interactions with your team. Identifying these values starts with introspection. Consider the moments when you felt most fulfilled or proud—what values were you upholding? Maybe it was integrity during a challenging decision, empathy when a team member faced personal struggles, or courage when leading your team through uncertainty.

To align your leadership approach with your personal values:

- List five moments in your career that made you feel genuinely accomplished.
- Identify the values you were expressing in those instances.
- Look for patterns to pinpoint your core values.

Philosophy Statement

Crafting a concise philosophy statement is like creating a personal tagline. This statement encapsulates your approach and values, serving as a reminder and a beacon for both you and your team. Here's how you can craft this:

- Reflect on what leadership means to you. Is it about guiding, inspiring, serving, challenging, or something entirely different?
- Combine your leadership meaning with your core values identified earlier.
- Keep it concise—no more than two sentences. Think of it as your leadership mission statement.
- For instance, "I lead by empowering my team to take ownership of their work, grounded in trust and driven by a collective pursuit of excellence."

Alignment With Organizational Culture

The effectiveness of your leadership is partly determined by how well it aligns with your organization's culture. Discrepancies here can lead to friction and hinder your ability to lead effectively. To ensure cohesion:

- Understand the core values and mission of your organization. This information is often found in company manifestos, mission statements, or corporate social responsibility reports.
- Assess how your leadership philosophy complements the organizational culture. Are there areas of strong alignment or potential conflict?
- Adapt your approach where necessary, without compromising your core values, to better fit the organizational context.

Evolving Your Philosophy

A static leadership philosophy is like a map that doesn't account for new roads or terrains; it quickly becomes outdated. As you grow and learn, your understanding of leadership will evolve. Embracing this evolution is key to remaining relevant and effective. This means:

- Regularly reflecting on your leadership experiences and the lessons learned.
- Seeking feedback from peers, mentors, and team members.
- Adjusting your philosophy statement to reflect your growth and new understandings.

Visual Element: Leadership Philosophy Worksheet

A worksheet can guide leaders through the process of defining their leadership philosophy. It could include sections for:

- Listing career-defining moments and associated values.
- Drafting a preliminary philosophy statement.
- Comparing personal leadership philosophies with organizational culture.
- Planning for regular reviews and updates to the philosophy statement.

Interactive Element: Values Identification Exercise

A values identification exercise prompts leaders to select values from a comprehensive list that resonate with them. This is followed by reflection questions to narrow down these values to their core few. This exercise can be facilitated in leadership development workshops or used individually.

Textual Element: Real-Life Leadership Philosophy Examples

A collection of leadership philosophy statements from diverse leaders across various industries may offer insight into how different values and approaches are articulated into coherent and impactful philosophies.

Defining your leadership philosophy is the first step in crafting your unique leadership identity. It requires deep reflection, honesty, and a willingness to grow. As you move through this process, remember that your philosophy is not just words on a page—it's a living, breathing guide that shapes how you lead, make decisions, and interact with your team. It's the groundwork upon which your leadership mosaic is built, piece by piece, into a masterpiece that is distinctly yours.

9.2. COMMUNICATING YOUR LEADERSHIP VISION

Creating and sharing a leadership vision that captivates and propels your team forward requires both clarity and passion. This vision not only outlines where you're steering the ship but also why it's a voyage worth taking. It's the beacon that guides your team through calm and stormy seas alike. Here, we will navigate through the process of crafting this vision, ensuring it resonates deeply, aligns with team objectives, and influences every decision made.

Vision Crafting

A compelling leadership vision begins with understanding what drives you as a leader. It's a reflection of your highest aspirations, not just for yourself but for your team and the broader organization. To start this process:

- Reflect on what success looks like in the long term. Consider the impact you want to have and the legacy you wish to leave.
- Think about the values and principles that are non-negotiable on this journey. These should be deeply embedded in your vision.
- Use vivid, engaging language to paint a picture of the future you're working towards. This should be something that excites and motivates, making the hard work ahead seem not just necessary but desirable.

Your vision should act as a guiding star, consistently guiding efforts and inspiring progress, no matter the challenges faced.

Effective Communication Strategies

Once your vision is crystalized, the next step is to communicate it in a way that ignites a shared passion within your team. Here are several strategies to ensure your message not only lands but resonates:

- Tailor your communication to your audience. Consider what aspects of your vision will speak most to your team's motivations and concerns.
- Utilize storytelling to make your vision relatable and memorable. Share personal anecdotes or hypothetical scenarios that illustrate the vision in action.
- Be present and authentic. Your team needs to see and feel your conviction. Your authenticity will inspire them to follow your lead.

Repeatedly communicating your vision in various formats—meetings, emails, and one-on-ones—helps reinforce its importance and keeps it at the top of everyone's mind.

Aligning Team Goals With Vision

For a leadership vision to truly take root, it must be woven into daily operations and long-term planning. This alignment ensures that every task, project, and goal contributes to the overarching vision. Achieving this involves:

- Breaking down the vision into actionable objectives. Each team or department should understand how their work directly contributes to the larger goal.
- Setting short-term goals that act as stepping stones towards the vision. Celebrating these milestones as they're

achieved reinforces the progress being made.
- Regularly reviewing team objectives and strategies to ensure they remain in sync with the vision. Adjust as necessary to stay on course.

This process not only clarifies the role each team member plays but also fosters a sense of ownership and commitment to the vision.

Role of Vision in Decision Making

A well-defined leadership vision also serves as a critical tool in decision-making. It acts as a filter through which options can be evaluated, ensuring that choices are consistent with the direction you're heading. To integrate your vision into decision-making:

- Before making significant decisions, ask how each option aligns with your vision. Will it move the team closer to or further from the envisioned future?
- Involve your team in decision-making processes where possible. This not only leverages diverse perspectives but also reinforces their commitment to the vision.
- Use your vision to prioritize. When faced with competing demands, focus on what advances your vision and delegate or delay what doesn't.

By consistently applying your vision to decision-making, you ensure that every choice propels your team toward the desired future, reinforcing the vision's relevance and guiding your journey forward.

Crafting and communicating a leadership vision is an ongoing dialogue—a narrative that evolves as goals are met and new challenges arise. It's a dynamic process that demands reflection, adaptation, and, most importantly, a deep connection with your team. Your vision is the promise of what you aim to achieve together; communicating it effectively is how you turn that promise into a shared mission, driving every action and decision toward making that envisioned future a reality.

9.3. THE IMPACT OF LEADERSHIP ON ORGANIZATIONAL CULTURE

Leadership as a Cultural Catalyst

In the dynamic world of organizational management, leaders play a pivotal role in shaping the culture within their purview. A leader's actions, decisions, and demeanor act as a mirror, reflecting values and norms that permeate the organization. This ripple effect, where leadership behavior influences the organizational ethos, underscores the power of leadership as a cultural catalyst. For instance, when leaders consistently prioritize transparency in their dealings, it fosters an environment where openness is valued and practiced at all levels.

Similarly, leaders' commitment to continuous learning sets a precedent, encouraging an organizational culture that values development and innovation. This dynamic interplay between leadership behavior and organizational culture highlights the importance of intentional leadership. Leaders must not only be aware of the culture they wish to cultivate but also actively embody the characteristics of that culture in their everyday actions.

Fostering a Positive Culture

Creating an environment that thrives on positivity, inclusivity, and innovation requires deliberate effort and strategies. Here are several approaches leaders can employ to foster such a culture:

- Promote Open Dialogue: Encourage an atmosphere where team members feel comfortable sharing their ideas and concerns. This could involve regular open forums or anonymous suggestion boxes, ensuring all voices are heard.
- Inclusivity at the Forefront: Make inclusivity a key component of your organizational culture by implementing policies and practices that embrace diversity. This could range from diversity training workshops to inclusive hiring practices.
- Celebrate Successes: Recognizing big and small achievements reinforces a positive culture. This could be as simple as a shout-out in a team meeting or as grand as an awards ceremony.
- Encourage Innovation: Allocate time and resources for team members to explore new ideas. This could take the form of innovation challenges or dedicated "experimentation days."

By integrating these strategies into daily operations, leaders can cultivate an environment where positivity, inclusivity, and innovation flourish. This will drive the organization toward its goals while also enhancing employee satisfaction and retention.

Modeling Desired Behaviors

The adage "actions speak louder than words" rings particularly true in the context of leadership and organizational culture. Leaders who model the behaviors they wish to see within their organization wield a powerful tool in shaping culture. This modeling goes beyond mere demonstration; it's about embodying the values and principles that define the desired culture.

For example, if collaboration is a cornerstone of the organizational culture, leaders can model this behavior by actively seeking input from various team members and departments before making decisions. Similarly, if resilience is a valued trait, leaders can share their experiences of overcoming challenges, highlighting the lessons learned and the importance of perseverance.

This approach not only communicates the desired behaviors to the team but also builds credibility and trust, as leaders are seen to "walk the talk." The consistency between what leaders say and do serves as a strong foundation for the organizational culture, encouraging team members to adopt these behaviors in their own work.

Sustaining Culture Through Change

Organizations are not static; they evolve and grow, often undergoing significant changes that can challenge the established culture. Sustaining and adapting the organizational culture through these periods of change is a critical leadership task. Here are some ways leaders can navigate this process:

- Reiterate Core Values: During times of change, reiterating the organization's core values helps remind team members of the foundational principles that remain constant. This can provide a sense of stability and continuity.

- Involve the Team in the Change Process: By involving team members in planning and implementing changes, leaders can ensure that the evolving culture aligns with the organization's values and goals. This collaborative approach also fosters a sense of ownership and engagement among team members.
- Communicate Transparently: Keeping the lines of communication open during transitions is crucial. Transparently sharing the reasons behind changes, expected outcomes, and any anticipated challenges can help mitigate uncertainty and resistance.
- Adapt Leadership Styles: As the organization evolves, leaders may need to adapt their leadership styles to meet new demands and challenges. This flexibility can be key in navigating change effectively, ensuring that the organizational culture remains vibrant and aligned with the organization's direction.

In conclusion, the role of leadership in shaping and sustaining organizational culture cannot be overstated. Through intentional actions, fostering positive environments, modeling desired behaviors, and skillfully navigating through changes, leaders have the unique opportunity to cultivate a culture that not only reflects their vision and values but also propels the organization toward its objectives. By doing so, they lay the groundwork for a resilient, inclusive, and innovative organizational culture that stands the test of time and change.

9.4. LEAVING A LASTING LEADERSHIP LEGACY

In leadership, the concept of legacy often conjures images of grand achievements and monumental contributions. However, a truly meaningful legacy is more nuanced, reflecting the depth of impact a leader has on their organization and its people over time. A legacy is about the values instilled, the growth fostered, and the culture nurtured—elements that endure long after a leader has moved on.

Defining Your Legacy

Initiating this reflective process involves a careful consideration of what you want to be remembered for. Is it for nurturing a culture of innovation, fostering diversity and inclusion, or perhaps for mentoring the next generation of leaders? Pinpointing the essence of your desired legacy requires a deep connection with your core values and a clear understanding of the difference you want to make. Here's how to start:

- Reflect on the changes you've initiated and the values you've championed within your organization.
- Consider the feedback you've received from peers and team members about your leadership style and its impact.
- Visualize the future of your organization and what foundational elements you believe should be sustained beyond your tenure.

Long-Term Impact on Teams

Strategies for imprinting a lasting impact are as varied as leaders themselves. However, certain practices stand out for their effectiveness in leaving a legacy that resonates:

- Mentorship: Actively seeking opportunities to mentor individuals not just in skills but in values and philosophies can mold the organization's future leadership.
- Development Programs: Establishing or supporting programs that encourage continuous learning and growth ensures the organization's commitment to development is ingrained in its DNA.
- Culture Building: Consistently reinforcing the cultural attributes you value through actions and decisions helps solidify them as enduring aspects of the organizational identity.

Measuring Your Legacy

While the influence of a leadership legacy can be profound, quantifying this impact presents a challenge. However, certain indicators can offer insights into the breadth and depth of your legacy:

- Feedback from Team Members: Regular feedback sessions can provide valuable insights into how your leadership is perceived and its effect on individuals and the team.
- Cultural Assessments: Evaluating changes in organizational culture over time can offer clues to the lasting impact of your leadership practices.
- Succession Success: A smooth transition of leadership and the continued success of the organization under new leadership can be strong indicators of a well-established legacy.

As you contemplate the legacy you wish to leave, remember that its true measure lies not in the accolades received or the milestones achieved but in the positive influence exerted on the lives of those you lead and the organization you serve. It's about creating a foundation that not only supports the current success but also fosters future growth and innovation.

The leadership journey is one of continuous evolution, where the legacy you leave becomes a testament to the values you've championed, the growth you've nurtured, and the culture you've cultivated. As we transition from the theme of legacy to the broader landscape of leadership evolution, we carry forward the understanding that a leadership legacy is not a destination but a continuous journey—one that shapes not just the future of your organization but the future of those you've had the privilege to lead.

10

CULTIVATING GROWTH—THE CONTINUOUS EVOLUTION OF LEADERSHIP

Imagine a professional athlete at the top of their game. They don't stop training the moment they win a championship; they double down, knowing their competition is always evolving, and so must they. Similarly, in leadership, the moment you stop learning is the moment you fall behind. This chapter focuses on the commitment to lifelong learning, a cornerstone for any leader aiming to stay relevant and effective in a rapidly changing world.

10.1. EMBRACING LIFELONG LEARNING IN LEADERSHIP

Commitment to Learning

Leadership isn't a static skill set but a dynamic range of abilities that grow and adapt over time. A true leader views every day as an opportunity to learn something new, whether it's a better way to motivate their team, a more efficient process, or insights into emerging industry trends. Consider incorporating a "learning hour" into your weekly schedule, dedicating this time to absorbing new information through articles, podcasts, or discussions with mentors. This habit not only broadens your knowledge base but also models the value of continuous learning for your team.

Learning Resources and Opportunities

The internet has democratized knowledge access, providing various resources across various platforms. From MOOCs (Massive Open Online Courses) offered by universities to short-form learning on platforms like LinkedIn Learning or Coursera, leaders have a wealth of knowledge at their fingertips. Additionally, attending industry conferences, workshops, and seminars not only aids in learning but also in networking with peers who can offer fresh perspectives and insights.

- Online Courses: Platforms like edX or Coursera offer courses on everything from leadership principles to specific technical skills taught by industry experts and university professors.
- Workshops and Seminars: Look for local or virtual workshops focusing on leadership development. These can offer interactive learning experiences and the opportunity to discuss real-life scenarios with peers.
- Reading Groups: Start a reading group within your organization focused on leadership books. This encourages collective learning and opens up avenues for discussing how these insights can be applied within your team.

Personal Development Plans

A Personal Development Plan (PDP) acts as a roadmap for your growth as a leader, laying out specific goals, the resources you'll use to achieve them, and timelines. To create an effective PDP, start by identifying areas for improvement or new skills you wish to acquire. Next, outline the steps needed to achieve these goals, including which resources you'll use and how you'll measure success. Regularly review and adjust your PDP to reflect your evolving goals and your organization's changing needs.

Learning From Experience

Experience remains one of the most potent learning tools, offering lessons that are often more impactful and enduring than theoretical knowledge. Reflecting on successes and failures provides invaluable insights into your leadership style, decision-making process, and resilience. Keep a leadership journal in which you document significant challenges you've faced, the decisions you made, and the outcomes. Reflect on these entries to identify patterns, learn from mistakes, and recognize successes. Dedicate time each week to jot down key decisions, challenges, and their outcomes. Use this as a tool for reflection and growth.

In a world that never stops changing, the leaders who stand out are those who never stop learning. They recognize that every experience, every piece of feedback, and every new piece of information is an opportunity to grow, not just as leaders but as individuals. By committing to lifelong learning, seeking out diverse resources and opportunities, creating personal development plans, and learning from experience, leaders can ensure they remain effective, relevant, and ready to tackle tomorrow's challenges.

10.2. SEEKING FEEDBACK FOR CONTINUOUS IMPROVEMENT

Creating a Feedback-Friendly Environment

In a world where change is the only constant, feedback emerges as a beacon, guiding leaders toward growth and adaptation. Creating a feedback-friendly atmosphere is pivotal, allowing for the free exchange of ideas and observations. Here, the goal is to cultivate a space where feedback is not only welcomed but eagerly anticipated for the growth opportunities it presents. To achieve this, consider implementing regular "Feedback Fridays," informal sessions designed for the open exchange of thoughts and ideas. Additionally, developing a "Feedback Charter" can set clear expectations and norms around feedback, ensuring everyone understands its value and approach.

- Feedback Fridays: Weekly sessions inviting open dialogue and feedback sharing among team members and leaders.
- Feedback Charter: A document outlining the norms, values, and rules surrounding feedback within the team or organization, crafted collaboratively to ensure buy-in.

360-Degree Feedback

The 360-degree feedback mechanism is a powerful tool, offering a panoramic view of a leader's impact through the eyes of their colleagues, direct reports, and even clients. This feedback model provides a rich tapestry of perspectives, highlighting strengths and areas for improvement. For successful implementation, start with a pilot program, selecting a small, diverse group to participate and provide feedback. This allows for adjustments to the process before a full-scale rollout. It's crucial to accompany this feedback with coaching or workshops to help leaders translate insights into actionable growth plans.

- Pilot Program: A trial run of the 360-degree feedback process with a select group, allowing for refinement of the process.
- Coaching and Workshops: Post-feedback sessions aimed at helping leaders understand their feedback and develop plans for growth.

Acting on Feedback

Once feedback is received, the real work begins. The process of integrating this feedback into one's leadership practice is where transformation takes root. Prioritize feedback based on its alignment with your personal development goals and the impact on your team's performance. Create an "Action Plan" for integrating feedback and setting specific, achievable targets for improvement. Regular reflection on this plan is essential, assessing progress and making adjustments as necessary. Remember, feedback is a gift, and acting on it demonstrates a commitment to personal and team growth.

- Action Plan: A detailed plan specifying the steps to be taken in response to feedback, including timelines and measurable outcomes.
- Regular Reflection: Scheduled times for reviewing progress on the action plan, allowing for adjustments and reevaluation of goals.

10.3. THE ROLE OF MENTORING IN LEADERSHIP DEVELOPMENT

In the dynamic landscape of leadership, the tradition of mentoring stands out as a time-honored avenue for personal and professional growth. Mentoring's value transcends the simple transmission of knowledge, fostering deep, reciprocal benefits for mentors and mentees alike. This nuanced relationship, rooted in trust and mutual respect, serves as a catalyst for unlocking potential and navigating the complexities of leadership.

Benefits of Mentoring

Mentoring is not a one-way street. It's a symbiotic relationship where both participants emerge enriched. For mentees, the immediate advantages include gaining practical advice, industry insights, and invaluable networking opportunities. They receive a tailored learning experience that accelerates their professional development and enhances their problem-solving skills. Mentors, on the other hand, benefit from fresh perspectives, the satisfaction of contributing to someone's growth, and the opportunity to refine their leadership and coaching skills. This reciprocal dynamic ensures the mentoring relationship adds value, reinforcing the mentor's own understanding and approach to leadership while guiding the mentee on their path.

Finding and Being a Mentor

Navigating the path to finding a mentor or becoming one begins with self-reflection. For those seeking mentorship, it's crucial to identify specific areas for growth and the qualities you value in a mentor. Networking events, professional associations, and even

LinkedIn can be fertile ground for finding a mentor whose experience and leadership style align with your aspirations.

Conversely, for leaders looking to mentor others, the first step is to make your willingness known. Communicate your interest in mentoring within your professional circles and on platforms where potential mentees might seek guidance. Building a productive mentoring relationship hinges on setting clear expectations, establishing open communication, and agreeing on goals. This foundation enables both parties to navigate the mentoring process effectively, ensuring a rewarding experience.

- Open Communication: Prioritize honesty and transparency from the outset. Discuss goals, expectations, and any potential challenges.
- Setting Goals: Collaboratively establish specific, achievable goals. This ensures both mentor and mentee are aligned and can measure progress.
- Regular Check-ins: Schedule consistent meetings to discuss challenges, celebrate achievements, and adjust goals as necessary.

Structured Mentoring Programs

Many organizations recognize the value of mentoring in leadership development and offer structured programs to facilitate these relationships. Participating in or establishing such a program within your organization can systematically expand the mentoring culture. These programs often provide guidelines, resources, and support to ensure successful mentoring relationships. They can match mentors and mentees based on complementary skills, interests, and goals, offering a structured framework that includes training for mentors, goal-setting sessions, and regular evaluations to monitor progress.

For leaders interested in creating a mentoring program, consider the following steps:

- Needs Assessment: Conduct an assessment to understand the specific development needs within your organization.
- Program Design: Outline the structure of the program, including the process for matching mentors and mentees, the duration of the mentoring relationships, and any formal training components.
- Monitoring and Support: Implement mechanisms to monitor the progress of mentoring relationships and provide ongoing support to participants.

Structured mentoring programs not only facilitate individual growth but also contribute to building a culture of learning and development within the organization.

Mentoring as a Legacy Activity

For leaders, mentoring is a powerful avenue for building a lasting legacy. It allows you to impart wisdom, share experiences, and shape the leaders of tomorrow. Through mentoring, you can ensure that your values, knowledge, and insights continue to influence your organization long after you've moved on. This legacy activity underscores your commitment to the growth and development of others, fostering a culture where knowledge is shared and potential is nurtured.

Mentoring is a testament to the belief that leadership is not about holding knowledge but about sharing it. It's about lifting others as you climb, guiding them through the complexities of their careers, and helping them to navigate their paths with confidence. In doing so, you not only contribute to the development of future leaders but also cement your own legacy as a leader who made a difference.

10.4. STAYING AHEAD OF LEADERSHIP TRENDS

In a rapidly evolving world, staying informed and ahead of leadership trends is not only advantageous; it's necessary for ensuring sustainable success and relevance. This section delves into strategies that enable leaders to keep pace with the changing landscape, ensuring their approach remains effective and their teams resilient.

Monitoring Leadership Trends

Keeping an eye on emerging trends and challenges ensures you're moving forward with purpose and preparedness. Regularly scanning reputable business journals, subscribing to industry newsletters, and engaging with thought leadership on platforms such as LinkedIn or Medium can provide a wealth of insights. Additionally, leveraging artificial intelligence tools that curate content based on your interests can streamline this process, ensuring you're always in the loop without overwhelming your schedule.

- Set aside dedicated time each week for trend analysis.
- Use technology to your advantage by employing content curation tools.
- Engage with the content critically, assessing its relevance and potential impact on your leadership style and organization.

Adapting to New Leadership Paradigms

The landscape of leadership constantly shifts, introducing new paradigms and technologies that can significantly enhance efficiency, communication, and team dynamics. Embracing these changes requires a mindset that sees adaptability as a strength. This might involve experimenting with new software tools that facilitate remote work or adopting more inclusive leadership practices that reflect the workforce's increasing diversity. The key is to continually remain open to experimentation, learning from successes and setbacks to refine your approach.

Experiment with new tools and methodologies on a small scale before full implementation.

Participation in Professional Networks

Engaging with professional networks, attending conferences, and participating in forums are invaluable for exchanging ideas and staying abreast of new leadership trends. These interactions offer a dual benefit: they not only expand your knowledge base but also enhance your professional network, opening doors to collaborative opportunities and partnerships. Prioritize attending events that are directly relevant to your industry or leadership interests, but also consider those that may offer a new perspective or challenge your existing viewpoints.

- Actively contribute to discussions and forums, sharing your insights and experiences.
- Seek out networking opportunities that align with your professional growth goals.
- Be open to forming connections outside your immediate industry for a broader perspective.

In navigating the complexities of modern leadership, the strategies outlined here serve as a compass, guiding leaders through the ever-changing landscape. By staying informed about leadership trends, embracing adaptability, actively engaging in professional networks, and fostering innovation, leaders can ensure they remain at the forefront of their fields, ready to lead their teams with vision and effectiveness.

As we conclude this exploration into the dynamic realm of leadership evolution, it's clear that a leader's journey is one of continuous growth and adaptation. The commitment to staying informed, embracing new paradigms, and innovating practices ensures not only personal development but also the sustained success and resilience of the teams and organizations we lead. As we transition from this chapter, we carry forward the understanding that the essence of leadership lies not in resting on past laurels but in striving for future excellence, constantly seeking new ways to inspire, engage, and lead those around us.

11

CRAFTING YOUR LEADERSHIP ACTION PLAN

Imagine standing at the edge of a forest. Each path represents a different aspect of leadership development, with various trails leading to distinct areas of growth. Crafting your leadership action plan is similar to mapping out the route you'll take through this forest. It's about deciding which paths to explore, which challenges to tackle, and what tools you'll need along the way.

Now, let's focus on setting goals that aren't just any markers on your map but are the guiding stars that ensure every step you take moves you in the right direction.

11.1. SETTING SMART LEADERSHIP GOALS

Clarity and Focus

As a leader, goals act as your road signs, guiding your decisions and actions. However, not all goals are created equal. Imagine deciding to 'improve leadership skills' without specifying what that looks like. That would be like setting out on a hike without knowing which mountain you're aiming to summit. This is where SMART goals come into play, ensuring your leadership objectives are Specific, Measurable, Achievable, Relevant, and Time-bound.

- **S**pecific: Your goal should be clear and focused. For instance, rather than aiming to 'improve communication,' target 'enhancing team meetings by incorporating structured feedback sessions.'
- **M**easurable: Attach numbers or indicators to track progress. If the goal is to enhance team meetings, a measurable indicator could be achieving an 80% positive feedback rate from team members on the effectiveness of meetings.
- **A**chievable: Assess resources and constraints to ensure your goal is realistic. Enhancing team meetings, for example, might require training on feedback techniques or allocating more time for each session.
- **R**elevant: Align goals with your broader leadership vision and organizational objectives. Improving team meetings should directly contribute to enhancing team performance or morale.
- **T**ime-bound: Set a deadline. Perhaps aim to achieve the 80% positive feedback rate within six months, providing a clear timeframe for action and evaluation.

Alignment With Vision

Every goal should relate to your overarching vision for leadership and the organization's objectives. This alignment ensures that your efforts contribute to a larger purpose. If your vision includes fostering a culture of continuous feedback, enhancing team meetings with structured feedback sessions directly supports this vision, creating a cohesive direction for your actions.

Measurability and Tracking

To navigate your leadership development effectively, you need a compass—that's where measurability comes in. Establishing clear metrics allows you to track progress and make informed decisions on whether to stay the course or adjust your approach. For the goal of enhancing team meetings, regular surveys or feedback forms can serve as tools to gauge the effectiveness of the new structure and content of the meetings.

Timeliness

A deadline acts as your finish line, motivating action and helping maintain focus. Goals can become open-ended aspirations rather than concrete objectives without a set timeframe. For instance, setting a six-month deadline to achieve the 80% positive feedback rate on team meetings introduces a sense of urgency and commitment, driving you and your team to implement and refine the new meeting structure actively.

Setting SMART leadership goals transforms vague aspirations into actionable plans, ensuring every effort contributes meaningfully to your growth and the success of your organization. By focusing on clarity, alignment, measurability, and timeliness, you position yourself to navigate the complexities of leadership development with confidence and precision.

11.2. IDENTIFYING RESOURCES AND SUPPORT

Navigating the complexities of leadership development requires more than just a well-crafted plan; it demands a network of support and access to resources that can fuel your growth. This section explores the pillars that uphold a successful leadership development strategy, focusing on mentorship, professional networks, developmental opportunities, and a robust support system.

Utilizing Networks

Professional networks and communities serve as a lifeline, providing not just resources and opportunities but also a sense of belonging to a larger ecosystem. Engaging with these networks can open doors to new ideas, partnerships, and personal and professional development avenues. Here's how you can maximize the benefits of professional networks:

- Active Participation: Don't just join; actively participate in discussions, attend events, and contribute your knowledge and expertise.
- Expand Your Circle: Regularly seek out new connections, but also deepen existing relationships within your network.
- Offer Value: Approach networking with a mindset of what you can offer, not just what you can gain. This reciprocal approach fosters stronger, more meaningful connections.

Building a Support System

The leadership journey can be challenging, making a strong support system invaluable. This system should encompass not just professional contacts but also personal connections that offer encouragement and feedback. Building this system involves:

- Identify Your Circle: Recognize the individuals who provide different types of support, from professional guidance to emotional encouragement.

- Cultivate Reciprocity: Ensure your relationships are built on mutual support and respect, where you are as much a pillar for others as they are for you.
- Open Channels of Communication: Maintain regular communication with your support network, sharing your successes and seeking advice during challenges.

A well-rounded support system acts as a safety net, ensuring that when the inevitable hurdles of leadership arise, you have a network to help you regain your footing and continue forward.

In sum, a successful leader's development hinges not just on personal drive and a well-defined action plan but also on the resources and support systems that surround them. By actively seeking mentorship, engaging in professional networks, accessing targeted development opportunities, and cultivating a strong support system, leaders can confidently navigate their development backed by a wealth of resources and a robust support network.

11.3. CREATING A TIMELINE FOR YOUR LEADERSHIP DEVELOPMENT

Navigating the vast terrain of leadership growth requires not just a compass but a map that marks where you've been and where you're headed. This map, your timeline, is unique to your path, reflecting both the aspirations you aim to reach and the milestones you'll celebrate along the way.

Realistic Planning

When sketching your timeline, realism is your ally. This means balancing what's aspirational with what's achievable, ensuring that your goals are neither too lofty to reach nor too modest to challenge you. Start by breaking down your overarching objectives into smaller, manageable tasks, each with its timeline. For instance, if enhancing team productivity is a goal, you might begin with implementing new communication tools, followed by team-building exercises, then regular feedback sessions—all spaced out over several months.

- Begin with the end in mind and work backward, plotting the major steps needed to achieve each goal.
- Allocate more time than you think you'll need for each task to account for unforeseen challenges.
- Prioritize tasks based on their impact and urgency, focusing on what will move the needle most.

Incorporating Milestones

Milestones serve as beacons of progress, illuminating your path and offering moments to reflect and recalibrate. They're not just achievements but checkpoints that offer insights into what's working and what might need adjustment. When mapping your timeline, identify key milestones that signify progress toward your larger goals. These could range from completing a leadership course to successfully mediating a team conflict, each marked on your timeline as a point of celebration and evaluation.

- Define clear criteria for what constitutes a milestone to avoid ambiguity.
- Space milestones evenly to maintain momentum and motivation.
- Celebrate each milestone, acknowledging the effort and learning that got you there.

Visual Mapping

A visual representation of your timeline can transform it from a concept into a clear, actionable plan. Visual mapping tools, whether digital apps or traditional whiteboards, allow you to lay out your timeline in a format that's easy to understand and adjust. These tools can enable you to:

- Color-code tasks and milestones for quick identification.
- Drag and drop items to easily adjust timelines and priorities.
- Share your timeline with mentors or team members for input and collaboration.

A visual map of your leadership development journey not only serves as a constant reminder of where you're headed but also inspires and motivates you to keep moving forward. It turns abstract goals into tangible targets, making the path to leadership growth clear and navigable.

Crafting a timeline for your leadership development is much like charting a course for an expedition. It requires a keen understanding of the terrain ahead, an appreciation for the milestones along the way, and the flexibility to navigate unforeseen obstacles. By plotting your course with realism, marking progress with milestones, allowing for adjustments, and bringing your journey to life with visual mapping, you equip yourself with a powerful tool for personal and professional growth. This timeline becomes not just a guide but a living document of your leadership evolution, capturing both the aspirations you strive towards and the achievements you'll undoubtedly accomplish.

11.4. MONITORING AND ADJUSTING YOUR PLAN

In the world of leadership development, crafting an initial plan is only the first step. The real magic lies in the ongoing process of evaluation, adaptation, and documentation. This dynamic approach ensures your growth strategy remains relevant, effective, and aligned with both your personal aspirations and the evolving needs of your organization.

Regular Review Sessions

Setting aside time for regular review sessions is like pausing to check your map and compass during a hike. These sessions are vital for assessing your progress toward your set goals and understanding the landscape of challenges you've encountered. Schedule these reviews with a frequency that matches the pace of your goals —monthly for short-term objectives and quarterly for longer-term aims. During these sessions, ask yourself:

- Have I moved closer to my goals?
- What obstacles did I encounter, and how did I navigate them?
- Do any goals need to be adjusted based on my progress or changes in my environment?

These questions foster a reflective mindset, encouraging a deep dive into your achievements and areas for improvement.

Feedback Integration

Feedback from mentors, peers, and team members is a goldmine of insights. It offers perspectives that might not be visible from your vantage point. Integrate this feedback into your leadership development plan by:

- Actively seeking feedback after key projects or milestones.
- Organizing regular feedback sessions with your mentor and peers.
- Creating a safe space for your team to share their observations and suggestions.

This feedback not only enriches your understanding of your leadership impact but also highlights areas for refinement or new opportunities for growth.

Documenting the Journey

Keeping a detailed record of your leadership development journey offers numerous benefits. It allows you to:

- Track your progress against goals.
- Reflect on the challenges faced and the strategies that proved effective.
- Celebrate achievements and learning along the way.

Consider maintaining a leadership journal or digital portfolio where you document your reflections, key learnings, feedback received, and adjustments made. This documentation will serve as a personal archive of your growth and as a resource for future reflection and learning.

By weaving these elements into your leadership development strategy, you create a dynamic and responsive plan that charts your growth path and adjusts to the terrain as you progress. This blend of planning, reflection, and adaptability underpins a truly effective approach to leadership development.

As we wrap up this exploration of crafting and refining your leadership action plan, remember that the essence of leadership lies not in the plan itself but in the action it inspires and the growth it fosters. Your plan is a living document, one that evolves with you as you navigate the complexities and opportunities of leadership. It's a tool for guiding your development, informed by feedback, shaped by reflection, and enriched by the journey itself.

Looking ahead, we'll delve deeper into these strategies' practical applications, exploring how they are applied in the real world of leadership challenges and opportunities.

12

PUTTING YOUR LEADERSHIP PLAN INTO ACTION

Imagine a captain at the helm of a ship, navigating through calm and stormy seas alike. The ship's progress depends not just on setting the right course but also on the captain's ability to adapt to changing conditions, inspire the crew, and maintain momentum toward the destination. Similarly, leadership's true test comes when you start implementing your plan, facing real-world challenges, and steering your team toward success.

12.1 45. TAKING THE FIRST STEPS: INITIATING CHANGE

Overcoming Inertia

Starting can often be the hardest part. It's like standing at the bottom of a hill, knowing you need to reach the top but feeling daunted by the climb. Inertia, that tendency to do nothing or to remain unchanged, is a common hurdle. To overcome this, focus on breaking down your goals into smaller, manageable tasks. If your goal is to improve team communication, start with something as simple as scheduling regular check-ins.

- Actionable Strategy: Schedule a 15-minute morning meeting every Monday to discuss weekly goals and any potential roadblocks.
- Why it Works: It creates a routine, making the task less daunting and easier to start.

Small Wins

Early successes fuel motivation. They're proof that you're moving in the right direction. Let's say you've decided to enhance your public speaking skills. Your first small win could be delivering a short, informal presentation to your team.

- Visual Element: Create a "Win Board" in your office or a digital version for remote teams where you can post these small victories. Seeing progress visually can be incredibly motivating.

Communicating Intentions

Change is more effective when it's a team effort. Openly sharing your leadership goals and the steps you're taking to achieve them can rally support from your team and stakeholders. For instance, if one of your goals is to foster a more inclusive workplace culture, communicate this intention in your next team meeting, explaining why it matters and how each team member can contribute. You could also host a workshop where team members can share their ideas and strategies for contributing to this goal. This will encourage buy-in and collective action.

Leveraging Early Learning

Every step you take toward your goals offers valuable lessons. Say, in your efforts to improve decision-making processes within your team, you tried a new approach that didn't pan out as expected. Rather than viewing this as a setback, see it as a learning opportunity. What went wrong? What could be done differently? Use these insights to refine your strategies moving forward. Try keeping a leadership diary where you jot down what you tried, what worked, what didn't, and why. This can be a powerful tool for reflection and adaptation.

By taking proactive steps toward your goals, celebrating small wins, sharing your intentions, and learning from each experience, you set the stage for meaningful change and growth. Remember, the first step might be the hardest but also the most crucial. It's where change begins.

Transitioning from planning to action is like shifting gears from theory to practice. It's where you test your strategies, refine your approach based on real-world feedback, and truly begin to see the impact of your leadership. Remember, the goal isn't to avoid obstacles but to learn how to navigate them effectively. Each challenge you overcome not only moves you closer to your goals but also builds your resilience and adaptability as a leader.

12.2. BUILDING MOMENTUM AND MAINTAINING FOCUS

The path to realizing leadership goals is like flying a plane. Maintaining a steady course requires both vigilance and effort. Consistency in these efforts propels the aircraft forward, cutting through the sky and making headway toward the intended destination. Similarly, in the pursuit of leadership development, daily commitment to growth activities, regardless of the sea's calm or tumult, builds momentum.

Consistency in Efforts

Think of consistency not just as repetition but as the rhythm that underlies a successful leadership practice. This rhythm, much like the heartbeat of a drummer in a band, keeps the entire ensemble moving together, setting the pace for progress. To foster this consistency:

- Start each day with a brief review of your leadership development goals, aligning your day's tasks with these objectives.
- Integrate leadership practices into your daily routines. For instance, if improving listening skills is a goal, dedicate part of your team meetings to practicing active listening.
- Use reminders or set specific triggers that cue you to engage in your leadership development activities, turning these actions into habits over time.

Prioritization

With the multitude of responsibilities vying for attention, prioritizing becomes not just a skill but a necessity. It's about distinguishing between what's urgent and what's important, focusing on activities that yield the highest impact on your leadership growth. For effective prioritization:

- Apply the Eisenhower Matrix: This time management tool is designed to help prioritize tasks by urgency and importance.

- Delegate tasks that others can do, freeing up space to focus on activities that significantly contribute to your leadership development.
- Regularly review your priorities, understanding that as goals evolve, what you prioritize might also need to shift.

Resilience

The journey toward leadership excellence is strewn with obstacles; resilience enables you to navigate these challenges without losing sight of your goals. Resilience is that inner reserve of strength that allows you to rebound from setbacks, learn from each experience, and emerge stronger. Cultivating resilience involves:

- Viewing challenges as opportunities for growth rather than insurmountable obstacles.
- Developing a strong support network of colleagues, mentors, and friends who provide encouragement and perspective.
- Practicing self-care to maintain your physical, mental, and emotional well-being, ensuring you have the energy and focus needed to pursue your goals.

12.3. CELEBRATING MILESTONES AND REFLECTING ON PROGRESS

Recognizing the progress made on the path to enhancing leadership skills demands both acknowledgment of achievements and a thoughtful reflection on the journey thus far. It's like climbers taking a moment to enjoy the view from a new height they've reached, appreciating both the terrain they've covered and planning their next steps.

Recognition of Achievements

Acknowledging milestones, both big and small, plays a pivotal role in not only motivating oneself but also in inspiring the team. It's a practice that reinforces the value of the effort put in and the strides made toward the ultimate goals. Here's how to effectively celebrate these milestones:

- Personal Acknowledgment: Set aside time to reflect on what achieving this milestone personally means for your growth as a leader. Perhaps it was leading a successful project or enhancing team communication. Recognize the skills you've developed or sharpened in the process.
- Team Celebrations: When milestones involve team efforts, celebrate them collectively. This could be through a team lunch or a simple acknowledgment in a team meeting. It's about creating moments recognizing team effort and fostering a sense of shared accomplishment.
- Public Recognition: Consider broader recognition within the organization for significant milestones. Highlighting these achievements in company-wide meetings or newsletters celebrates success and sets a benchmark for leadership excellence.

Reflective Practices

Reflection serves as the mirror through which the nuances of each leadership experience can be understood and appreciated. It's about looking back to dissect what worked, what didn't, and how different approaches can enhance future endeavors. Here are some reflective practices that can enrich this process:

- Journaling: Keeping a leadership journal offers a private space to document thoughts, feelings, and observations about your leadership journey. Regular entries following key milestones or during times of change can provide insightful retrospectives on personal growth and leadership development.
- Debrief Sessions: Organize a debrief session with your team after completing a significant project or reaching a milestone. This structured discussion focuses on what was learned, the challenges faced, and the successes achieved. It encourages collective reflection and learning.
- Mentor Discussions: Engage with your mentor to reflect on recent achievements and the journey. Their external perspective can offer invaluable insights into your growth and areas for further development.

Sharing Successes

Transparency in sharing your successes and the lessons learned through your leadership journey fosters a culture of growth and development. It encourages others to pursue their development with vigor and openness. Here's how to share effectively:

- Storytelling in Meetings: Use team or organization-wide meetings as platforms to share stories of your leadership journey, focusing on both the successes and the challenges overcome. This narrative approach makes the sharing relatable and engaging.
- Mentor and Peer Discussions: Regularly discuss your progress with mentors and peers. These conversations can be a source of mutual learning and inspiration, offering both support and constructive feedback.

- Leverage Digital Platforms: Consider sharing your leadership journey and achievements on professional networks like LinkedIn for a broader reach. This will not only celebrate your milestones but also encourage a community of learning and support among professionals.

In the grand mural of leadership development, celebrating milestones and reflecting on progress are brushstrokes that add depth and color to the narrative. These practices not only mark the journey but also enrich it, ensuring that each step taken is acknowledged and utilized as a stepping stone for future growth. By recognizing achievements, engaging in reflective practices, adjusting goals, and sharing successes, leaders can continue to navigate their development with insight, adaptability, and a shared sense of accomplishment.

12.4. SCALING YOUR LEADERSHIP IMPACT

In effective leadership, the ability to magnify one's influence and create a resonant impact far beyond the immediate team marks the transition from manager to visionary leader. This section delves into potent strategies that enable leaders to extend their influence, thereby shaping broader organizational and community landscapes.

Expanding Influence

The scope of a leader's influence should not be confined to the boundaries of their immediate team but should extend to encompass larger organizational objectives and even community-wide goals. Achieving this requires a proactive approach:

- Networking with Purpose: Actively seek connections outside your immediate circle, particularly with individuals leading other teams or departments. This broadens your perspective and creates opportunities for collaborative initiatives that can have a wider impact.
- Volunteering for Cross-Departmental Projects: By participating in projects that cut across different parts of the organization, you position yourself as a leader with a broad organizational view, not just a departmental one. This can significantly amplify your influence across the organization.
- Community Engagement: Extend your leadership beyond the organization by getting involved in community projects or industry forums. This not only broadens your impact but also enhances your leadership skills through diverse experiences.

Strategic Delegation

Empowering others is a pivotal aspect of scaling your leadership impact. Strategic delegation involves assigning responsibilities, ensuring task success, and fostering team members' growth and development.

- Identify Strengths and Growth Opportunities: Match tasks with team members' strengths or areas where they seek growth. This ensures that delegation is not just task allocation but a developmental tool.
- Provide Autonomy: Trust your team with autonomy over how they complete tasks. This fosters a sense of ownership and responsibility, which is crucial for developing leadership capacity within the team.

- Feedback and Support: Ensure that delegation is followed by constructive feedback and the necessary support. This transforms every delegated task into a learning opportunity, contributing to the team's overall growth.

Thought Leadership

Positioning yourself as a thought leader amplifies your leadership voice beyond the confines of your organization, impacting the broader industry or community. Here are some pathways to establishing thought leadership:

- Speaking Engagements: Share your insights and experiences at industry conferences or webinars. This not only broadens your influence but also positions you as an expert in your field.
- Writing: Contribute articles or blog posts to reputable industry publications or platforms. This allows you to share your vision and leadership philosophy with a wider audience.
- Mentorship: Offering mentorship to individuals outside your immediate team or organization can significantly extend your leadership influence. As you guide and support emerging leaders, you contribute to shaping the future leadership landscape.

Sustainability and Legacy

The ultimate goal of scaling your leadership impact is to create sustainable practices and a lasting legacy that positively influences the organizational culture and sets a benchmark for future leaders. This involves:

- Institutionalizing Best Practices: Work toward embedding successful leadership practices into the organization's fabric. Whether it's innovative project management techniques or effective communication strategies, ensure these practices are documented and adopted widely.
- Fostering a Culture of Continuous Improvement: Lead by example in promoting a culture where seeking improvement and embracing change is the norm. This will create a legacy of adaptability and resilience.
- Building a Leadership Pipeline: Actively identify and develop potential leaders within the organization. This not only ensures continuity of leadership but also cements your legacy as a leader who contributed to building the organization's future leadership.

Scaling your leadership impact requires a deliberate and thoughtful approach. This approach goes beyond achieving immediate goals to fostering growth, development, and innovation at every level. By expanding your influence, delegating strategically, establishing yourself as a thought leader, and focusing on sustainability and legacy, you set the stage for a leadership impact that resonates across time and space, inspiring current and future generations.

12.5. NURTURING FUTURE LEADERS

In the dynamic realm of leadership, nurturing future leaders leads to forward-thinking and sustainable success. Organizations find their enduring strength and innovative spirit through the careful cultivation of burgeoning talent. Here, we explore the multifaceted approach to fostering the next generation of leaders, ensuring the vitality and continuity of leadership excellence.

Mentorship and Coaching

Mentorship and coaching are at the core of developing emerging leaders. This personalized guidance is akin to providing a map and compass to a traveler embarking on an uncharted path. It's not merely about imparting knowledge but fostering a relationship that encourages exploration, questions, and growth.

- Personalized Guidance: Tailoring the mentorship to the mentee's aspirations and challenges ensures relevance and impact, much like customizing a training regimen for an athlete to enhance their specific strengths and address their weaknesses.
- Structured and Informal Sessions: Balancing structured sessions with informal interactions allows for both focused learning and the spontaneous exchange of ideas, mirroring the way a skilled craftsman alternates between meticulous planning and creative improvisation.

Development Opportunities

Creating and facilitating development opportunities for potential leaders is about setting the stage for growth, challenge, and discovery. It involves curating experiences that stretch their capabilities, much like pushing an artist to explore beyond their comfort zone to create something truly remarkable.

- Project Leadership: Assigning leadership roles in projects provides hands-on experience in managing tasks, teams, and outcomes, offering a real-world laboratory for honing leadership skills.
- Cross-Functional Assignments: Encouraging participation in cross-functional teams exposes future leaders to diverse

perspectives and challenges, broadening their understanding of the organization and enhancing their problem-solving skills.
- Leadership Rotations: Implementing a rotation program where emerging leaders can experience different organizational roles and departments fosters adaptability and a deep organizational understanding.

Recognition of Potential

Spotting and affirming others' leadership potential is like a gardener recognizing the promise in a budding plant. It's an act of faith in their capacity to grow and flourish, providing the encouragement and resources they need to thrive.

- Talent Spotting: Actively look for individuals who demonstrate initiative, curiosity, and the ability to inspire and mobilize others. This proactive talent spotting ensures that potential leaders are identified early and nurtured appropriately.
- Affirmation and Encouragement: Regularly affirming the potential you see in individuals serves as a powerful motivator, encouraging them to pursue leadership development with confidence and determination.
- Development Plans: Collaborating with potential leaders to create personalized development plans acknowledges their unique path to leadership, offering a structured approach to their growth.

Building a Leadership Pipeline

Building a robust leadership pipeline is an investment in the organization's future. It ensures a steady flow of capable leaders ready to step into roles as needed. It's about building a reservoir of talent that can sustain the organization through transitions, growth, and challenges.

- Comprehensive Talent Management: Integrating leadership development into the broader talent management strategy ensures that nurturing future leaders is a priority across the organization, not just within isolated departments.
- Succession Planning: A thoughtful succession planning process that identifies and prepares individuals for key leadership roles guarantees that the organization remains resilient in the face of change, much like a well-prepared ship weathers a storm.
- Continuous Learning Culture: Cultivating an organizational culture that values continuous learning and development sets the foundation for a dynamic leadership pipeline. It ensures that emerging leaders are always expanding their skills and perspectives, ready to meet the demands of tomorrow.

In nurturing future leaders, the goal is to foster an environment where potential can flourish, guidance is readily available, and challenges are seen as opportunities for growth. It's about looking beyond the immediate needs of the organization to prepare for a future that is vibrant, innovative, and led by individuals who are not only skilled and knowledgeable but also adaptable, visionary, and deeply committed to the success of their teams and the broader organization. In doing so, leaders today lay the groundwork for a legacy of leadership that endures, evolves, and continues to inspire long into the future.

12.6. EVOLVING YOUR LEADERSHIP FOR FUTURE CHALLENGES

In the ever-changing leadership landscape, the concept of evolution plays a pivotal role. It's about recognizing that what brought success yesterday might not necessarily apply tomorrow. This evolution is not just about adapting to change; it's about proactively preparing for it, ensuring that as leaders, we remain not just relevant but ahead of the curve.

Innovative Thinking

Addressing future challenges requires a departure from conventional thinking and embracing innovation as a core leadership quality. This involves looking beyond the immediate and the obvious and exploring novel solutions to problems. Imagine a situation where traditional approaches to customer engagement are failing. A leader with a penchant for innovative thinking might explore cutting-edge technologies like augmented reality to create more immersive experiences. Ways to foster innovative thinking include:

- Hosting regular brainstorming sessions with your team, encouraging out-of-the-box ideas.
- Implementing a 'fail fast, learn fast' approach to experimentation, where innovative ideas are tested quickly, and lessons are drawn from the outcomes.
- Partnering with startups or innovation hubs to infuse fresh perspectives and ideas into your strategies.

Legacy of Learning and Adaptability

Ultimately, the legacy a leader leaves behind isn't just about the successes achieved but also about the culture of learning and adaptability instilled within the organization. This legacy ensures that even in the leader's absence, the team or organization possesses the resilience and agility to face future challenges head-on. Creating this legacy involves:

- Documenting and sharing your learning journey, making it accessible for future leaders.
- Recognizing and rewarding learning and adaptability within the team, making these qualities a cornerstone of your leadership legacy.
- Mentoring future leaders, imparting not just knowledge but also the importance of adaptability and continuous learning.

As one navigates the complexities of leadership, embracing continuous learning, adaptability and flexibility, innovative thinking, and cultivating a legacy of learning become crucial. These qualities ensure that leaders are not just reacting to changes but are proactively preparing for them, ready to leverage opportunities and navigate challenges with confidence.

With this focus, leaders can ensure they're not just surviving the tides of change but thriving, setting a course for others to follow. The path ahead is filled with unknowns, but with a steadfast commitment to evolving and growing, leaders can forge ahead, creating a brighter future for themselves, their teams, and their organizations.

As we close this exploration of evolving leadership for future challenges, we're reminded that the essence of leadership lies in its capacity to grow, adapt, and innovate. Through a commitment to continuous learning, adaptability, innovative thinking, and fostering a legacy of learning, leaders can ensure they're equipped not just for the challenges of today but for the opportunities of tomorrow. This readiness enhances personal and professional growth and contributes to crafting an enduring impact that resonates through the ages.

Moving forward, the journey continues, with each step offering a chance to learn, adapt, and innovate.

CONCLUSION

As we draw the curtains on this transformational leadership journey, I reflect on the path we've tread together. From the initial steps of discovering and honing our leadership styles to the intricate dance of building and nurturing high-performing teams and steering these teams through the winds of change, we've traversed a landscape rich with insights and opportunities for growth. This book has been a vessel, guiding you through the complexities of leadership, with each chapter illuminating the way forward.

Self-awareness has been central to our exploration. It's the cornerstone of effective leadership, allowing you to glimpse into your own psyche, understand your strengths and areas for improvement, and appreciate the profound impact you wield over those you lead. Self-awareness is not just a tool for introspection but a compass guiding your leadership journey.

We've also delved into the critical role of emotional intelligence in forging strong, empathetic connections with team members. This emotional acumen is what transforms a workplace from a mere collection of individuals to a cohesive, thriving community. It's about more than just achieving targets; it's about creating an environment where people feel valued, understood, and motivated.

The landscape of leadership is ever-evolving, marked by new challenges and opportunities. Embracing continuous learning and adaptability is not optional but essential. The leaders who thrive are those who remain curious, open to new ideas, and ready to pivot when the situation demands. Your leadership action plan, tailored from the insights and strategies shared in these pages, is your roadmap. It's a call to action, urging you to put theory into practice and begin the tangible work of shaping your leadership legacy.

Speaking of legacy, I invite you to contemplate the mark you wish to leave on your team and organization. Leadership is an odyssey replete with trials and triumphs. It's about the impact you make, the growth you inspire, and the paths you pave for those who will follow. Your legacy is the echo of your leadership, resounding long after you've moved on.

I encourage you to embrace this leadership journey with all its vicissitudes. Step forward with determination, armed with the knowledge that the challenges you face are merely stepping stones on the path to greatness. And as you journey, I urge you to share your stories of leadership, the trials you've overcome, the wisdom you've garnered, and the impact you've made. In sharing, we build a community of leaders united in our pursuit of excellence and inspired by each other's journeys.

Thank you for joining me on this voyage. Your commitment to refining your leadership is a testament to your resolve to make a difference. Continue to pursue excellence in your role, for in doing so, you not only elevate yourself but also those you lead. Remember, the journey of leadership is not a solo endeavor but a shared voyage enriched by the stories we tell and the lives we touch.

May your leadership journey be fulfilling, your impact profound, and your legacy enduring. Here's to the leaders we are and the leaders we aspire to become.

KEEPING THE GAME ALIVE

Now that you have everything you need to excel in leadership, it's time to pass on your newfound knowledge and show other readers where they can find the same guidance and support.

Simply by leaving your honest opinion of "Effective Leadership Skills for Managers" on Amazon, you'll show other aspiring leaders where they can find the tools to thrive and pass their passion for leadership forward.

Thank you for your help. Leadership is kept alive when we share our knowledge – and you're helping me to do just that.

Scan the QR code below to leave your review:

By sharing your experience, you not only contribute to the growth of others but also solidify your own understanding of what it takes to be a great leader. Every review counts, and yours could be the one that lights someone's path towards effective leadership. Thank you for being part of this continuous journey of learning and leading.

REFERENCES

Active listening: Techniques, benefits, examples. Very Well Mind. https://www.very-wellmind.com/what-is-active-listening-3024343

Be Friendly, not friends: Maintaining professional distance. Linkedin https://www.linkedin.com/pulse/friendly-friends-maintaining-professional-distance-key-g-moore

Effective time management for leaders. Maven. https://maven.com/articles/time-management-strategies

5 Powerful things happen when a leader is transparent. Forbes. https://www.forbes.-com/sites/glennllopis/2012/09/10/5-powerful-things-happen-when-a-leader-is-transparent/

5 steps in the change management process. HBS Online https://online.hbs.edu/blog/post/change-management-process

5 ways leaders enable innovation in their teams. Forbes. https://www.forbes.com/sites/glennllopis/2014/04/07/5-ways-leaders-enable-innovation-in-their-teams/

Fostering inclusion and engagement: Strategies for success in remote teams. Talent Mgt. https://www.talentmgt.com/articles/2023/12/04/fostering-inclusion-and-engagement-strategies-for-success-in-remote-teams/

How diversity can drive innovation. HBR. https://hbr.org/2013/12/how-diversity-can-drive-innovation

How leaders can get the feedback they need to grow. HBR. https://hbr.org/2023/03/how-leaders-can-get-the-feedback-they-need-to-grow

How to build your leadership brand on social media. LinkedIn https://www.linkedin.-com/advice/0/what-best-ways-build-your-leadership-brand-social-h4krf

How to communicate clearly during organizational change. HBR. https://hbr.org/2017/06/how-to-communicate-clearly-during-organizational-change

Inclusive leadership: Steps to take to get it right. CCL. https://www.ccl.org/articles/leading-effectively-articles/when-inclusive-leadership-goes-wrong-and-how-to-get-it-right/

Leadership development plan: Template and example. Valamis. https://www.valamis.com/hub/leadership-development-plan

Leading by example: The power of authentic leadership in management. Economic Times. https://m.economictimes.com/jobs/c-suite/leading-by-example-the-power-of-authentic-leadership-in-management/articleshow/104592158.cms

Managing a remote team - Top challenges and solutions. View Sonic. https://www.viewsonic.com/library/business/managing-a-remote-team-top-challenges-and-solutions/

Managing multicultural teams. HBR. https://hbr.org/2006/11/managing-multicultural-teams

New managers can communicate better - 5 proven ways. Lsag Global. https://lsaglobal.com/blog/5-ways-new-managers-can-communicate-better-with-their-team/

19 advantages of mentoring in the workplace. Insala. https://www.insala.com/blog/key-benefits-of-mentoring

9 Tips for good leaders to improve their persuasion skills. Elevate Corporate Training. https://www.elevatecorporatetraining.com.au/2019/11/25/9-tips-for-good-leaders-to-improve-their-persuasion-skills7

Strategies to Build a More Resilient Team https://hbr.org/2021/01/7-strategies-to-build-a-more-resilient-team

Powerful diversity workplace statistics to know for 2023. Instride. https://www.instride.com/insights/workplace-diversity-and-inclusion-statistics/

Situational leadership: What it is and how to build it. BetterUp. https://www.betterup.com/blog/situational-leadership-examples

Six strategies to maintain employee motivation. Forbes. https://www.forbes.com/sites/rebeccaskilbeck/2019/02/12/six-strategies-to-maintain-employee-motivation/

10 powerful feedback models to use at work. Join. https://join.com/recruitment-hr-blog/feedback-models

The importance of self-care for managers. Corporate Wellness. https://www.corporatewellnessmagazine.com/article/the-importance-of-self-care-for-managers

The 7 step process for managing underperforming employees. Eddy. https://eddy.com/the-7-step-process-for-managing-underperforming-employees/

Top 7 decision-making tips for managers. BDC. https://www.bdc.ca/en/articles-tools/entrepreneurial-skills/be-effective-leader/7-decision-making-tips-managers

12 practical ways to ensure effective communication. Forbes. https://www.forbes.com/sites/forbeshumanresourcescouncil/2021/01/21/12-practical-ways-to-ensure-effective-communication-among-multicultural-team-members/

20 email best practices for leaders. Rapid Start Leadership. https://www.rapidstartleadership.com/20-email-best-practices-for-leaders/

Unconscious bias: A silent menace to leadership and how to overcome. Linkedin. https://www.linkedin.com/pulse/unconscious-bias-silent-menace-leadership-how-overcome-rajdeep-dutta

Virtual meetings: 10 best practices for remote teams. Switchboard. https://www.switchboard.app/learn/article/virtual-meeting-guide

What is cultural intelligence and why is it key to business? Nationwide. https://www.

nationwide.com/business/solutions-center/management/what-is-cultural-intel
ligence

Why self-reflection is key in great leadership. Waldenu. https://www.waldenu.edu/
online-masters-programs/ms-in-leadership/resource/why-self-reflection-is-
key-in-great-leadership

Why emotional intelligence is crucial for effective leadership. Forbes. https://www.
forbes.com/sites/forbesbusinesscouncil/2023/07/25/why-emotional-intelli
gence-is-crucial-for-effective-leadership/

Why learning is the key to leadership. Forbes. https://www.forbes.com/sites/willia
marruda/2023/10/08/why-learning-is-the-key-to-leadership/